AROUND AND ABOUT THE CUSTOM HOUSE

This book is published with
the special assistance of
AIB CAPITAL MARKETS

and

AN ROINN COMHSHAOIL

DEPARTMENT OF THE
ENVIRONMENT

Around and about the Custom House

Jane Meredith

with an introduction by
Maurice Craig

FOUR COURTS PRESS

ACKNOWLEDGEMENTS AND CREDITS

ACKNOWLEDGEMENTS

Some years ago Brendan O'Donoghue, Secretary of the Department of the Environment, commissioned Eve McAulay to collect images depicting the story of Gandon's great masterpiece, the Custom House, and its surrounds during its two centuries of existence. This book has developed from Eve's work and so to her, and to Brendan O'Donoghue, who commissioned me and whose idea it was, my first thanks are due.

For their kindness in reading the draft text, and their advice, support and encouragement throughout, I would especially like to thank Dr Edward McParland and Dr Maurice Craig; and to all those others who gave me their time and shared their knowledge, enthusiasm and expertise I would like to express my heartfelt thanks.

Lastly, publication would not have been possible without the assistance of the Department of the Environment and AIB Capital Markets, and I thank them for the opportunity which their joint sponsorship has given me.

Jane Meredith

LIST OF ILLUSTRATIONS

Custom House. **45** *Dublin Obsequies of Lord Mayo: Landing the Coffin at the Custom House Quay.* From *Illustrated London News*, 4 May 1872. **46** Rose Barton (1856-1929). *Departure of 4th Dragoon Guards from Custom House Quay, June 18, 1891.* Watercolour. 29.85 x 52.07 cms. **47** Joachim Gerstenberg. *Guinness Boats at Custom House Quay.* **48** *Carlisle, now O'Connell, Bridge, Dublin, before the 1880 rebuilding,* showing original obelisks. Trade card of William Law, goldsmith & jeweller, 1 New Sackville St, Dublin. **49** *Shipping at Burgh Quay & Eden Quay,* with Carlisle Bridge & Bachelor's Walk in the foreground, c.1870. **50** *Custom House with the original Butt Bridge, 1879,* designed to swivel. **51** *View looking west along Eden Quay* showing the swivel Butt Bridge, 1879. **52** *View looking east from Bachelor's Walk* (taken c.1891), with O'Connell Bridge, the old swivel Butt Bridge and the Loopline Bridge. **53** View from Burgh Quay of the new Butt Bridge and the Loopline. **54** James Horan. *The Custom House.* Drawing, from *25 Views of Dublin* by James Horan, commissioned by the Office of Public Works. **55** *Custom House Crescent & Riverside Station.* Taken from P. Abercrombie's *Dublin of the Future,* 1922. **56** Harry Clarke. *The Last Hour of the Night.* Frontispiece to *Dublin of the Future,* 1922. **57** James Gandon (1742-1823). *Elevation of Beresford Place, 1790.* City Hall, Dublin, Wide Streets Commissioners' Map. **58** Plan*: Custom House Revenue Stores & Docks in Dublin.* Made by John Taylor in 1824. **59** *Liberty Hall after Bombardment in Easter Week, 1916.* **60** *Liberty Hall and Custom House, 11 May 1991.* **61** *Busaras,* taken from Custom House Roof, January 1997. **62** *Part-plan of Docks Development to date (February 1997).* **63** *Cartoon from* 40 Years of Dublin Opinion, 1962. **64** S.F. Brocas (c.1792-1847). *View of the Corn Exchange, Burgh Quay & Custom House.* Engraved by H. Brocas (c.1790-1846). Published 1 July 1820, by J. Le Petit, for his *Book of Views of Ireland,* 20 Capel St, Dublin, & by Wright & Bell, Duke St, Bloomsbury, London. 24.5 x 40 cms. **65** *52p stamp marking the 200th Anniversary of the Custom House.* Issued 11 April 1991, to coincide with Dublin's tenure of the European City of Culture title. **66** *Back of current Central bank of Ireland £10 note.* **67** *Front of £1 Consolidated bank 'Ploughman's' note.* **68** *Back of £1 Consolidated bank 'Ploughman's' note, showing the Custom House.* **69** *Detail from Irish Hospitals Sweepstakes Pageant, 1938.* **70** *Irish Hospitals Sweepstakes Pageant, 1938.* **71** Attributed to Reverend Calvert Jones. *Earliest known photograph of Custom House, 1843.* **72** *The Liffey, Custom House & Eden Quay, Dublin.* Print taken from Thomas Nelson & Sons' *Views in Ireland,* c.1871. **73** Robert Mannix (1841-1907*). The Port of Dublin & Custom House, 1883.* Oil on canvas. 91.44 x 152.4 cms. **74** Rose Barton (1856-1929). *The Custom House before the Rebellion.* Signed but undated. Watercolour. 27.3 x 34.93 cms. **75** Flora Mitchell (1890-1973). *The Last of the Arklow Schooners, undated.* Illustration from *Vanishing Dublin,* 1966. Ink & watercolour on paper. 47.6 x 36.2 cms. **76** Alethea Garstin. *Guinness's Boat.* Undated. Oil on panel. 23.5 x 33.02 cms. **77** Stephen Wiltshire (b.1974). *The Custom House.* **78** *Map:* Detail of Ordnance Survey map of Dublin City 1:20,000. 15th Popular edition (1992).

ILLUSTRATION CREDITS

The author and publishers thank the following owners (and unnamed private collectors) for permission to use illustrations:

An Post **65**; Central Bank of Ireland **66**; Central Bank of Ireland and Ian Whyte of Whyte International Auctioneers and Valuers, Dublin **67, 68**; Mr Myles Christian **53**; Dr Maurice Craig **47**; Custom House Docks Development Authority **41, 62**, Dr John de Courcy **59**; Department of the Environment **21**; Dublin Civic Museum **48**; *Dublin Opinion* **63**; Dublin Port Board **23**; Fr Browne SJ Collection **69, 70**; Gorry Gallery **5, 24**; James Horan and the Office of Public Works **54**; Irish Architectural Archive **32** (Alfred Jones Biographical Index), **34**; Irish Film Archive **35**; John Johnson (Author's Agent) Ltd **77**; The Council of King's Inns **16-18**; Milmo-Penny Fine Art Gallery **76**; National Gallery of Ireland **2, 3, 6, 7, 9, 27, 75**; National Library of Ireland **1, 22, 26, 28, 49, 50, 51, 52, 64, 72**; National Maritime Museum Greeenwich and Dublin Port Board Archives **71**; National Museum of Ireland (the drawing is on loan to Dublin Civic Museum) **10**; Office of Public Works **13, 14, 15, 19, 29, 31, 33, 37, 39, 60**; Ordnance Survey of Ireland **78**; Sotheby's **46**; Trinity College Dublin **42, 43, 45, 55, 56**; Weidenfeld & Nicolson Archives **74**.

PHOTOGRAPHIC CREDITS

Audio-Visual and Media Services, Trinity College Dublin **42, 43, 45, 55, 63**; David Davison of Davison and Associates Ltd **10, 11, 12, 20, 21, 23, 32, 40, 44, 48, 57, 61, 69, 70, 73**; Padraig Ó Flannabhra **25**.

INTRODUCTION

Maurice Craig

Ever since it was built, the Custom House has been the most admired of Dublin buildings. Never mind that Henry Grattan called it 'a building of the sixth rate in architecture...' and 'a blemish in the eye of the island'. Politicians are not usually good judges of contemporary art, nor are they on oath on such occasions; and Grattan had an axe to grind. Since then the consensus has been that the Custom House is, in Manning Robertson's words, 'the glory of Dublin'. Even during the period when such buildings were badly out of fashion, its reputation has held.

There are good reasons for this. It was, more than most, self-consciously intended by its sponsors, men of taste and power, to draw attention to itself and to stand before the world as an emblem of the Kingdom of Ireland. Unlike most public buildings it was free-standing: you could walk right round it, admiring it from different angles. All four fronts, exceptionally, invited your attention, and all were highly finished. The decorations were virtually at eye-level, demanding to be looked at and appreciated. The tower and dome were to be a sea-mark no less than a landmark: the nodal point where the internal economy of Ireland and of Dublin confronted that of the world outside.

The statues on the skyline, and especially the bravura achievements of arms on the four corners, were designed to elevate the spirit as well as to please the eye. You might perhaps not bother to distinguish Neptune and Mercury from Industry and Plenty surmounting the central river-front portico, or those of the four continents in similar positions on the landward side, or even to notice that the arms over the pavilions, with their lions and unicorns, were not those of the royal house but of the country itself, still less, perhaps, to decipher exactly what is afoot in the busy sculpture filling the pediment. But you could not fail to appreciate, if only unconsciously, the justice with which these ornaments are placed, and their contribution to the profile of the building as a whole. It was, and it remained, unequivocally a statement. But – a statement of *what*?

There is a paradox in the fact that whereas the great architectural achievements of the last twenty years of the eighteenth century are associated in our mind with the partial legislative independence achieved by what we call 'Grattan's Parliament', the powerful group, headed by John Beresford, who were instrumental in so beautifying Dublin as a capital were out of sympathy with Grattan, as he was with them, and ten years after the Custom House was finished the kingdom of Ireland was finished and done for and had ceased to exist, largely as a result of the machinations of Beresford and his friends. But our instinct is right, all the same. Those twenty years were a period of unprecedented vitality, and with vitality comes, inevitably, conflict. Some of the energy went into politics and some of it into architecture. The architecture, as sometimes happens, has lasted better than the politics.

It is difficult for us to realise that at the end of the eighteenth century the parliament, the law courts and the revenue were housed, in Dublin, in much greater splendour than their counterparts in London. London was, of course, larger and more important than Dublin (though by a much smaller margin than later became the case). The difference was that, by 1800, Dublin had modernised itself and London had not. This was no accident: it was the result of deliberate policy, and the iconography of the Custom House makes this very explicit. Not only do the principal rivers of Ireland appear, along with the Atlantic Ocean, as the keystones, but the harp, as the national emblem, is conspicuous wherever you look, and in three sizes: the big ones on the shields between the lions and the unicorns, then the middle-sized ones on the frieze of the south portico, and finally the tiny harps, no bigger than a man's hand, on the necking of the columns, beautifully carved and meticulously undercut. They may not be much noticed by the casual passer-by, but they were taken note of by the designers of the stone piers which, a century later, were put in place to support the altogether lamentable, though inevitable, railway bridge. The piers were furnished with doric or tuscan columns in imitation, and, rather frugally, on the pier nearest the river, and there only, enriched the capitals with little harps, leaving the others plain.

A glance at the map shows that, like other such buildings in other European cities, the Custom House stands at the end of a long straight street: in this case Gardiner Street which leads to the development by Beresford's friends and allies, the Gardiner family, at and around Mountjoy Square. (Before it fell on evil days it was comparable to the splendid street which, under various names, runs from Merrion Square to Leeson Street Bridge.) But there is a departure from the norm, in that the exits and entrances from the square are not in the centres of the sides, as usually in Paris or London, but in the corners: a pattern which is repeated again and again in Dublin – at Rutland (Parnell) Square, at Merrion and Fitzwilliam Squares, and even at St Stephen's Green.

On the landward side the Custom House faces a crescent: again a common classical feature and one which was to be repeated a few years later at Hardwick Place facing St George's Church.

But, because of the position of the Custom House on the frontier between the residential area and the port, this pattern is, as it were, half-hearted. Gardiner Street culminates, as it had to do, on the building's central portico and not on the dome. Abbey Street (which was there already) comes in slantwise from the west, while to the east there was, from the beginning, close up to the building, the dock and its accompanying warehouses. The crescent of Beresford Place, domestic in character, is there all right, but the full hemicycle was never built and never intended. Only in our own time was the figure completed by the making of Memorial Road, by which time conditions had changed out of all recognition.

This raises the question, which may seem meaningless at first but is nevertheless teasing: where is the front door? Obviously, you will say, in the centre of the river front. But, at least within living memory, and probably for long before that, hardly anybody has been seen to go in or out this door. (This is true of several notable Dublin buildings: the Bank of Ireland for obvious reasons, the College of Surgeons, Holles Street Hospital, the Moyne Institute in TCD and others.) I have counted, in or near the river-front alone, at least seven doors or apparent doors, none of which, we may be sure, was John Beresford's habitual mode of entry. The river-front, in short, is largely for show, and none the worse for that.

The sumptuous suite of rooms, so resented and so ridiculed,

in which John Beresford installed himself, was in the western part of the north range, the part most convenient to town, and, we do well to remind ourselves, a part which faces north.

Eighteenth-century people did not care for sunlight. They knew it was bad for their books and furniture and thought it was bad for their complexions. (We now know that they were quite right.) All the corridors in the Custom House, which Gandon had put on the sunward side of each range, were, in the restoration of the 1920s, switched to the north, and the same thing happened at the Four Courts as well. Many a civil servant must have sweltered in summer as a result, especially since the six niches in the river front had been opened out as windows.

The entrance under the south portico is grand indeed, but that under the north portico is an even more carefully considered piece of architecture: under cover yet out of doors, more suitable for a private entrance and with special appeal to the connoisseur.

We are apt to forget, when we look at the early prints and paintings showing the river at Custom House Quay and City Quay crowded with shipping, how very much larger ships have been in the last hundred years than they were then. Even the small coasters of 600 tons or so, which until recently loaded Guinness' stout in barrels at the Custom House, took up half the length of the river-front, while the overnight Liverpool passenger ships of the B&I, which berthed further downstream, though very moderate in size, were as long as the whole of that facade. This, and more particularly the increased depth of water which they needed, is the reason why the surroundings of the Custom House are now so unrecognizably different from what they were when it was built.

Carlisle Bridge (the predecessor of O'Connell Bridge) was exactly contemporary with the Custom House. It connected, for the first time, the two fashionable quarters on the north and south Sides, and it sterilised the river all the way up to the Four Courts and beyond, making the quays, as quays, redundant, and therefore free to be redeveloped as an amenity. The same thing is happening now, downstream from the Talbot Memorial Bridge, and for the same reasons.

Every building which is in use or occupation begins to undergo alterations and adaptations, and sometimes even mutilations, from the moment it is commissioned. The Custom House is no exception, and it is arguable that, if we disregard the almost unthinkable disaster of 1921, it has got off more lightly than many. People who work in a building soon get into the habit of not seeing it, and of regarding it as simply a convenience to do as they like with. Governments have always behaved badly in this respect, but not worse than the churches, and perhaps less extravagantly than private owners.

It is unlikely that John Beresford's grand suite of private apartments in the north-west corner can long have survived his departure. No doubt they were soon appropriated as offices, and we can be sure that a good deal of cutting about and adaptation took place elsewhere in the interior. How, for example, could the numerous doors in the south range have been effectively controlled? And what about all those doors or apparent doors behind the two arcades – a dozen of them at the least? Some time before 1914 the eastern arcade had been glazed in. This was such a grossly visible mutilation that it is hard to see how it was allowed to happen. It provided very little extra accommodation. But it was easily remedied in the post-fire restoration.

The closing of the open arcades of the east block must have taken place when the original Custom House Dock fell into disuse and was superseded by those further down the river.

As originally built, there were fairly massive chimney-stacks, judiciously placed and intended to be 'read', though, by the usual conventions of the time, artists such as Malton tended to omit them. Other artists picked and chose among them, putting in those which seemed to help the composition and leaving out the rest. As the century wore on, extra fireplaces were inserted here and there, and favoured occupants had their own little 'pirate' chimney-stacks poking up through the roof, not, perhaps, so strikingly as in certain public buildings in Paris, such as the Bourse, but none the less making the roofline look, in places, quite bristly. All these disappeared in the restoration of 1929, along with the main stacks. Yet, even as recently as a few years back, I recall seeing one of these maverick or piratical stacks sticking up out of the south-east pavilion (and photographs bear this out). Whether it had managed to survive the holocaust, or had sprouted up again as weeds do when the effect of the weedkiller has worn off, is an interesting speculation.

More serious is the fact that the main stacks made a valuable contribution to the silhouette, and this is now lost. The tower and dome have always been open to criticism for the discrepancy of scale and the abruptness of their irruption. But, as Dr McParland has observed, this criticism loses its force when the front is seen, as it nearly always is, in a raking view. And the reason is this: as soon as the spectator moves off axis the statues detach themselves on one side of the tower, as did the high roof of the Long Room on the other, and they, as well as the stacks, gave the dome the visual support which it needed. But, though the statues were, mercifully, replaced at last in the most recent restoration, the Long Room roof has been long gone. And, of course, the darker colour of the reconstructed tower and peristyle is a blemish regrettably beyond repair. But things might be a great deal worse.

The original dispositions of the central block stretching from the river frontispiece to the corresponding part on the north were, from the beginning, somewhat anomalous. The Long Room (which was, by the way, not long at all but almost exactly square) was on the first floor. And neither the system of lobbies and staircases to the south, nor the equally elaborate system on the north, with its grand flying staircase, led at all directly to it. In the reconstruction of the 1920s the central block disappeared completely, and in its place are two parallel blocks with a light-well between them. There is a fairly grand staircase slightly to the north of where the old one was. The worst of the fire damage was in this part, because the wind was blowing from the south-east, and the destruction of the original staircase, which must have somewhat resembled Chambers' 'Navy' staircase at Somerset House (destroyed in the second world war but restored) is probably the greatest loss in the interior. It is only on this side, especially in the central and western sections of the north wall, that traces of the fire can still be seen from outside, scrupulously preserved in the recent restoration.

By contrast, and for the same reason, and also because of the materials used, the system of lobbies under the dome was surprisingly little damaged. The internal architecture resembles in character Gandon's House of Lords lobbies in Westmoreland Street. The main difference is that the main space is an octagon rather than a circle. But whereas the House of Lords lobbies have been open to and enjoyed by the public for many years, hardly anyone (and this includes, I suspect, most of the staff working in the building) has ever seen this part of the Custom House. This is partly because it does not lead from anywhere important to anywhere else. Matters were not improved by the flooring over of the central ground-floor space, in the ceiling of which there had been a large octagonal opening through which the more highly decorated domed first-floor space was intended to be, and had been, visible. Happily this has now been remedied.

The natural isolation of this area has made it possible to cut it off from the working part of the building, and to reveal it once more as a space for public benefit and enjoyment and as a setting for a discreet display of material illustrating the history of the building; but mostly, we must hope, to be looked at for itself, as architecture.

Two major disasters (some would say three) have befallen the Custom House during the course of its life. The terminal stations at Amiens Street and Westland Row had been in existence for the best part of half a century before it was decided, with, it is only fair to say, great hesitation and reluctance, to link them by the Loopline Bridge. It was inevitable that there should be communication between the main lines to Drogheda and Belfast on the one side and Dunlaoghaire (Kingstown) and Wexford on the other. Nor could a bridge at that level fail to ruin the view of the Custom House from upstream. (The first Butt Bridge, which had been in existence since 1879, was visually inoffensive.) It is less certain that the river had to be crossed at that particular point. During the early 1970s, CIE and the planning authorities were seriously considering re-routing the railway to the east, and if the junction with the Wexford line were to be made a quarter of a mile or so beyond Pearse (Westland Row) Station, this would give a much easier curve of larger radius and do away with the visual blight. Perhaps the new Custom House Docks developments have closed off that course for ever. Or perhaps not: for ever is a long time.

The second great disaster was of course the fire of 1921, about which not much need be said. It was no doubt a military necessity and it was a military success. But it is to be hoped that Michael Collins and his staff, or at least some of them, were visited, while planning this operation, by some such misgivings as assailed the allied command when they were planning the assault on Monte Cassino in 1944. Enough has already been said to show that as much was done as could be done by the lights of the time, to remedy the appalling destruction and to minimise the loss. Nevertheless, looking at the photograph of the dome peristyle taken after the fire, it is difficult not to won-

der whether it was really as unsafe as at the time it was claimed to be, and could not have been carefully taken down, strengthened from inside, and re-erected, as, I am sure, would have been done in the 1980s, had they had the chance. The damage to the four statues can hardly have been mainly due to the fire, since the flames were blown away from them and the statue on top, of Hope (or of Commerce, for the accounts vary) survived and was replaced, as were, triumphantly and as creditable modern reinstatements, the other four.

The erection of the new Liberty Hall in the 1960s would hardly, we must believe, have been permitted in the 1990s. Though a respectable building in itself, it is wildly out of scale with its neighbours. The example of Michael Scott's Busaras, a well-mannered building of 1953 which wears its age remarkably well, was there to be followed. It is not unknown for buildings, even ambitious buildings, of the 1960s to have a short life. So some now living may yet see the Custom House restored to its dominant role.

The story, during its 200-year life, has been of a constantly changing background, of setting and of activities. Even above Butt Bridge there was a good deal of shipping until the railway bridge made this impossible, but not till 1930-32 was the swivelling bridge replaced by its balustraded successor. Liberty Hall, which had started life in the 1820s as the Northumberland Family and Commercial Hotel, was taken over by Jim Larkin's ITGWU in 1912, and, as we all know, was bombarded by the *Helga* in Easter Week of 1916. Her aim must have been very precise, since the Custom House was not hit. But Liberty Hall was soon repaired and lasted in that form till, as we have seen, replaced by the building we have now.

Where Busaras is now, there was until the late 1940s, a range of warehouses of brown brick, possibly by the famous engineer John Rennie. But most conspicuously there was, to the east, at that time an unsightly hutted camp of extra accommodation.

This was partially screened by the railing, punctuated by rather handsome stone piers, nineteenth-century in date but designed to harmonise with Gandon's architecture. These disappeared, to my regret, when Memorial Road was made.

By the 1960s, the most frequent and pleasing activity at Custom House Quay had ceased: the Guinness traffic. The Brewery had taken to shipping on its own account in 1913, when it bought a second-hand steam collier, the *W.M. Barkley*. It had soon acquired three more such ships, the *Carrowdore*, the *Clareisland* and the *Clarecastle*. *Carrowdore* and *Clarecastle*, two uncommonly graceful ships, shared the work with the newly-built *Guinness* from 1931 onwards. They were 'fed' by a fleet of steam lighters with names taken from places near Dublin such as Clonsilla, Sandyford and Castleknock, which plied between Victoria Quay and the Custom House. Three of these were required to fill one of the seagoing ships. They had funnels which could be hinged down, and non-condensing engines, so that the procession of three plumes of steam, in line astern, was a familiar sight. Their passage had to be carefully timed to match the tide, so that while there must be enough water under their keels there would still be headroom to enable them to pass under the bridges.

The stout was in huge barrels which were handled by the ships' own lifting gear: steam winches and derricks. To protect the barrels from damage there were large round leather cushions four or five feet in diameter. Transport of stout round the city was in the hands of Richardsons of Tara Street, whose waggons, immaculately decked out in Guinness colours, were hauled by pairs of magnificent draught horses with burnished brasswork on their harness.

In the early fifties the *Clarecastle* and *Carrowdore* were replaced by the *Lady Grania* and the *Lady Gwendolen*, and in 1963 the *Lady Patricia* succeeded to the *Guinness*. In 1977 the

system was changed from loading and unloading barrels (by this time metal barrels) to pumping in and out of the ships' tanks. The *Patricia* was converted to this system, and the *Miranda Guinness* built to it. They usually berthed at City Quay. But in March 1993 the brewery ceased shipowning and reverted to consigning their product in other people's vessels. For the rest, the most constant users of this part of the quays have been the Irish Lights tenders: *Granuaile*, *Isolde*, *Atlanta* and the rest. But now they berth further downstream at Sir John Rogerson's Quay.

Ships, being built of perishable materials, have much shorter lives than buildings: shorter, even, for the most part, than those of men. The Custom House has seen many ships come and go, and not a few buildings as well. The most recent arrivals are those of the Financial Services Centre, an impressive tripartite composition, which counterpoints a group of convex facades to the larger concavity of the Beresford Place–Memorial Road curve. This is the setting in which, for the immediately foreseeable future, we now see the Custom House, as different from the original setting as though we were to see some great liner such as the *Aquitania*, first at the landing-stage in her home port of Liverpool, and then against the backdrop of Manhattan.

Many years ago I wrote that the Four Courts and the Custom House seemed to express the masculine and feminine aspects of Gandon's temperament. I have been teased and mildly ridiculed for this ever since, no doubt by people who had in mind a Freudian interpretation of the contrasted shapes of the two buildings. But that was not at all what I was thinking of. I was thinking much more of Schumann's description of Beethoven's Fourth symphony standing between the Eroica and the Fifth 'like a slender Greek maiden between two Norse giants'– a kind of critical discourse which is rather out of fashion at present. I still think I had a point. The Four Courts is rough in texture where the Custom House is smooth; heroic where the Custom House is lyrical; challenging in stance where the other is conciliatory and charming. It is, perhaps, significant that whereas, in the way that St Paul's and the Palace of Westminster figure as emblems of London, or the Eiffel Tower of Paris, this role, for Dublin, has been most often played by Nelson's Pillar or by the Four Courts: never by the Custom House. She is older, as was famously written of the Mona Lisa, than the rocks among which she sits: looking always outwards on a changing world, and retaining, through all the vicissitudes of her experience, an aspect of unfaltering serenity.

A NEW CUSTOM HOUSE FOR DUBLIN

The story of James Gandon's beautiful Custom House has many parts. The illustrations in this book have been chosen to depict just a few of them and are concerned not only with the Custom House itself, but with aspects of life around it.

The Old Custom House, which Gandon's was to replace, ceased to function as such in 1791, when its successor opened for business. It was situated approximately where the Clarence Hotel now stands, on the south bank of the River Liffey, to the east of Essex (now Grattan) Bridge. At that time Essex Bridge, which had been built by George Semple between 1753 and 1755, to replace an earlier bridge on the same site, was the last bridge before the sea. A glance at Rocque's map of 1757 (ill. 8) confirms the distance which merchant seamen had to sail to reach the Old Custom House. Among seamen it was not a popular journey as the approach to the quay was rocky and space so limited that the vessels had to moor several abreast. Unlike the business and merchant community centred around the Castle and Christ Church Cathedral, who were opposed to the move eastwards, a Custom House nearer the sea would have been welcomed by the seamen.

Our first illustration, an attractive tinted engraving (ill. 1) depicts Essex Bridge and, on its far side, on the south bank of the river, with the ships' masts clustered in front of it, the Old Custom House of 1707, designed by Thomas Burgh (who also designed Collins Barracks, the magnificent Old Library at Trinity College and Dr Steevens' Hospital). By the time the engraving was made in 1784 the building of Gandon's Custom House further downstream was well under way.

Following close upon the building of the new Custom House came Carlisle (now O'Connell) Bridge (ills. 48 & 49), opened in 1795 and also designed by Gandon. This meant that never again would tall-masted ships be able to sail up the river Liffey as far as Essex Bridge; any depiction of their presence there would indicate a date no later than 1791, when the foundation stone for Carlisle Bridge was laid.

2   James Malton, *Marine School, Dublin*, 1796

James Malton (*c.*1761-1803) is well known in Ireland for his aquatint plates of Dublin, which were collected into one volume entitled A Picturesque and Descriptive View of the City of Dublin, and published in 1799. In his Preface to this book James tells us that 'the entire of the views were taken in 1791, by the Author', but it seems almost certain that he then returned to London, where he worked up his material for publication. In

his original watercolour drawing (for his aquatint of 1796); (ill. 2) Malton shows, on the left, the Marine School as Gandon himself would have seen it, as he sailed up the Liffey for the first time, in 1781, to begin his great Dublin career. The authorship of this substantial, chunky building, with its more elaborate wings (one of which, the east, can be seen in the picture) is uncertain. It has been attributed to Thomas Ivory (1732-86) and Thomas Cooley (1740-84), but neither has been confirmed.

The School, originally called the Marine Nursery, prepared

1   (facing page) Essex Bridge (now Grattan Bridge) in 1784

3 The Custom House: a detail from Malton's *Marine School*

boys both for the merchant marine and the Royal Navy. Started at Ringsend in 1766, it moved to this site on Sir John Rogerson's Quay in 1773, where it stayed until 1872, when fire destroyed much of the building and it transferred to other premises.

It is of interest to note how built-up the quayside was in 1796, for it can be fairly safely assumed that these buildings were authentic and not invented by Malton; he is renowned for his meticulously accurate portrayals of the Dublin architectural scene, with, it must be admitted, an occasional degree of idealization.

The drawing shows, as many subsequent ones in this book will, the busy seagoing traffic on the river, indicative of the healthy state of the city's imports and exports business. The large sailing ship on the right of the picture would probably

4 The Custom House : a detail from Berger's *Marine View*

have been towed a good distance down from the quays until, with more room to manoeuvre, her sails could be unfurled.

In the distance, on the horizon, is Gandon's Custom House (detail: ill. 3). True to form, far away as it is, Malton's attention to detail has been scrupulous. Edward Smyth's soup-tureen chimney is missing from the south-east pavilion, as it is in Malton's watercolour of the Custom House (ill. 9). This, surely, could not have been a deliberate omission? The most likely explanation is either that these decorative chimneys, so reminiscent of those on William Chambers' beautiful Casino at Marino, were not added until later, or that Malton did not receive the drawings from Gandon in time to include them.

Johann Kristian Berger was born at Linköping in Sweden in 1803. He began his art studies in 1825 and, in the ensuing years, visited Ireland, England, France and Holland. He became painter to the Royal Swedish Court in 1841, and drawing teacher to the childen of King Oscar I. He specialized in shipping subjects and his seascapes and harbour views were inspired by Turner's work.

Like Malton, Berger has chosen for the oil painting shown overleaf a view of the Custom House as seen from the river, although from a point slightly further upstream. Here any similarity with Malton's work ends. This is a 'mood' piece, dramatic and somehow eerie, the bright patch of very blue sky contrasting with the swirling, brooding clouds on the right,

5   Johann Khristian Berger, *Marine View off Dublin, c.*1839

shafts of sunlight catching the sails of one boat and the prow of another, while the dark water is lit by a fiery glow.

The two foreground sailing ships are well observed and painted in some detail, even down to cargo being loaded up the gangplank of the ship on the left. However, the Custom House in the distance, half in light and half in shadow (detail: ill. 4), does not show the same attention to detail as Malton's.

Berger exhibited this painting in London in 1839, together with one other, entitled *Moonlight in Dublin Bay*, the present whereabouts of which is unknown.

JAMES GANDON

James Gandon (1742-1823; ill. 6) was forty when he landed in Ireland for the first time, in April 1781, to begin work on the Custom House, the first of the great projects with which he was to be involved in the ensuing years. Not much employed as an architect in England, he had supplemented his income there by print-making and publishing. Although thoroughly competent, there was little in his work to suggest the peak of excellence which he was to achieve in Ireland. With the Custom House, the House of Lords extension (now the entrance to the Bank of Ireland at the top of Westmoreland Street), the Four Courts and the King's Inns, he was to change the face of Dublin and embellish it with buildings which ranked among the best in Europe.

At the age of 15 Gandon joined the distinguished architectural practice of William Chambers, becoming his first pupil. Although Chambers never came to Ireland, he was responsible for the exquisite Casino at Marino, Charlemont House (now the Hugh Lane Gallery), and the Chapel and Examination Hall of Trinity College. Gandon himself had not travelled abroad, but there can be no doubt that he

6 (above) Horace Hone, *James Gandon*, *c.*1807

23

7 G. Stuart, *John Beresford*, c.1789-93

tect for the new Custom House. At his instigation, and with great secrecy, for many were opposed to the Custom House being moved downriver, Gandon produced rushed drawings and, one month later, in January 1781, was given the commission.

The site chosen for the new Custom House was on virgin land, half a mile downriver from the old one (sites ringed in ill. 8). Poorly drained, and close to the sea, it was inundated at spring tides, and laying the foundations posed a severe problem for Gandon. He relates how he went about the job: 'The great expense of preparing the piles, and the very long time it would take to drive so great a number as would be required, presented a strong objection to the use of them. I therefore gave directions to have a grating of Memel timber prepared, the timber to be one foot square, to have the upper ones notched down three inches in the ground pieces, which were to be bedded on a layer of cut heath, the whole ground being first correctly levelled; the interstices of the grating to be filled in with hard sound stock bricks, up to the level of the timbers, swimming in mortar composed of pounded roach lime and mortar well mixed … over which was laid four-inch fir plank fastened down on the grating with oak trennels…'.

Great credit must go to Gandon for the way he tackled this task, a feat of superb structural engineering. Many troubles have beset the Custom House throughout the years, but sinkage and cracked foundations have not been numbered among them.

Because of the opposition of so many to the site chosen, work got under way as inconspicuously as possible. Beresford laid the foundation stone in August 1781 'without any formality'; four weeks prior to this, when the foundation trenches were opened, there had been great fears of riots. Gandon recalls 'an ominous gathering of many hundreds of the populace', when 'Whiskey and gingerbread were in great demand. It was apprehended that

acquired his neo-classical tastes, and his preference for Roman antiquity, as well as his appreciation of fastidious masonry, from the years spent with his eminent master. How did it come about that Gandon was commissioned as architect for the new Custom House? Lord Carlow (later Lord Portarlington, for whom Gandon was to build Emo Court, in Co. Laois), was one of a circle of friends who enjoyed convivial Sunday morning *conversazioni* at the house of the artist Paul Sandby, in London. It was Gandon's introduction to this circle which heralded his subsequent career in Ireland, for it was here that Lord Carlow introduced him to John Beresford (ill. 7). Beresford, as First Revenue Commissioner, played a leading part in the selection of the archi-

8 (facing page) John Roque, Map of Dublin, 1756 (detail)

9 James Malton, *The Custom House, Dublin,* 1793

a riot would ensue, and that the trenches would be filled up: such was not the result; on the contrary, they amused themselves by swimming in them.'

A year and four months after this event the foundations were completed and work on building the new Custom House could begin.

The north elevation of the Custom House to-day is almost entirely in accordance with Gandon's early water-colour drawing (ill. 10), with the exception of the dome above the central portico, about which he later changed his mind.

That the south facade differs from the original, so faithfully represented by Malton (ill. 9), is not due to Gandon's change of plan but to the great fire of 1921. In Malton's drawing it can be seen that originally niches alternated with windows on the first floor, over the arcades, and the drum and colonnade of the dome were of the same pale Portland stone as the rest of the front facade. After the fire these were rebuilt in Ardbraccan limestone which, unfortunately, is becoming even darker with the passing years. Just visible behind the dome, in Malton's drawing, is the roof of the Long Room, which was destroyed by the fire and not replaced.

As mentioned before, Malton has not included the ornamental urn on the west elevation, but the coats of arms and the four statues over the front portico are all in place. However, he did not get the statues quite right; under a magnifying glass it can be seen that Carlini's two outer statues, Mercury and Neptune, have swapped places!

10 James Gandon, *Custom House, north elevation*

11 Coat of arms
12 Pediment and dome, from the riverfront

SCULPTURAL DECORATION

From the start Gandon planned a programme of sculptural decoration for his Custom House designed not only to complement and link its architectural components, but to proclaim, firmly but discreetly, Ireland's freedom to conduct her own trading affairs, unencumbered by British restrictions. Beresford would have stressed the importance of this approach in the early days, when discussing the proposed project with Gandon in London.

So it is that the coat of arms (ill. 11), although crowned, and supported by lion and unicorn, contains the harp of Ireland and not the shield of the House of Hanover; harp and English rose alternate in the delicate carving round the column capitals and, in the pediment, Hibernia and Britannia embrace; the relief carving on the wide portico friezes portrays, instead of the traditional *bukrania* (sculptured ox skull), hearty cattle heads, with flaring nostrils, supporting swags of hide, to symbolise Ireland's beef and tanning trade, while another larger harp inhabits a roundel above each swag (ill. 12). All around the building, over the main entrances, the rivers of Ireland, avenues of her trade, are personified in the form of carved keystone heads, laden with the produce of their courses, while inclusion of the Atlantic Ocean asserts Ireland's right to trade far afield. This right is also asserted in the four statues above the north portico, Europe, Asia, Africa and America, while the four over the south portico, Mercury, Plenty (with her cornucopia), Industry (with her beehive) and Neptune, symbolise the rewards of an industry which is served by a speedy maritime service. Meanwhile, from her lofty perch on the dome, Commerce presides over them all.

Of the three men employed to carry out the sculptural work on the Custom House, Agostino Carlini (d.1790), Thomas Banks (1735-1805) and Edward Smyth (1749-1812), it was Smyth, the Irish carver, who was to gain Gandon's highest approbation. Delighted with the excellence of his work, and with his understanding of scale, which coincided with his own, Gandon was to give him the lion's (and the unicorn's!) share of the work, but Smyth was still an unknown quantity when Gandon set out for Ireland and he took the precaution of securing the services of Banks and Carlini before he left England.

Banks, whom Gandon had known in London, carved the figures of the four continents, Europe and Asia, Africa and America (ills. 13-15), on the north portico. A group of drawings, on loan to the Custom House from the King's Inns Library, relates closely to the statues of Asia, Africa and America (ills. 16-18), but a comparison between the executed statues and the drawings would seem to suggest that sculptor and artist were not one and the same. Some scholars believe that Gandon's friend Paul Sandby was himself responsible for the drawings as, in the initial stages, he assisted Gandon in accumulating proposals for the Custom House statues.

Banks' carvings contain an extraordinary amount of detail which, unfortunately, cannot be fully appreciated from a distance. Smyth had a far better idea of the scale and amount of detail needed to achieve the greatest effect from afar.

Agostino Carlini was also known to Gandon in London, where his work had included carving riverine heads for Sir William Chambers, Gandon's old master, at Somerset House. In the end he carved only two figures for Gandon, Mercury and Neptune, the two outer ones on the south portico (ill. 12), as well as designing the pediment sculpture, which was carved by Smyth.

Edward Smyth, Gandon's favoured sculptor, was responsible for all the carving except that which has already been mentioned; so

13 Asia   14 Africa   15 America

his were the coats of arms, the ornamental urns, the riverine heads, the statues of Industry and Plenty over the south portico and Commerce on the dome, the delicate relief carving on the column capitals, the robust cattle on the portico friezes and the carving (to Carlini's design) of the pediment sculpture.

Gandon and Smyth, as has also been said, had the same ideas on scale and would have agreed that 'It's the look that counts.' Gandon's drum and dome (which owe much to Christopher Wren's Greenwich Hospital domes of 1696) seem out of proportion when seen head-on, but viewed from a raking angle, as when

13-18 Statues of Asia, Africa and America with designs

16 Asia   **17** Africa   **18** America   **19** Statue of Commerce

approaching up the river, the dome relates perfectly to the fore-shortened facade below. Similarly with the lion and unicorn on the monumental coats of arms (ill. 11). A contemporary observer, writing in 1786, criticized the beasts, remarking that 'like a book, whose preface is larger than its text, [they] may be said to be all head and no body'. At that early date it is likely that the coats of arms were still in the process of being carved; no doubt he changed his tune once they were in situ.

Smyth's fourteen riverine heads are one of the particular joys of the Custom House and, in their slightly more sheltered positions, have weathered the years, and the fire, reasonably well. Even though they all have curly beards (except, of course, Anna Livia, the only woman among them), no two are alike; there is, for instance, a cheerful one (the Bann), a grumpy one (the Foyle), some handsome ones (the Suir and the Shannon), some not so handsome ones (the Barrow and the Nore), a clear-eyed one (the Lee), a cross-eyed one (the Blackwater) and one bearing upon his brow a date of great historical importance (the Boyne).

Another survivor, the twelve-foot high statue of Commerce (ill. 19), is shown here, down from her pedestal for cleaning and restoration during the most recent conservation programme (she received new fingers and a new nose!), before being returned to her eyrie.

TOP (l. to r.)
Lagan, Atlantic, Suir,
Shannon, Barrow

MIDDLE
Blackwater, Boyne,
Bann, Foyle, Slaney

BOTTOM
Liffey, Nore, Lee, Erne

20 Edward Smyth's riverine heads

SOME NINETEENTH-CENTURY PAINTINGS

Patrick Byrne (1783-1864), who is reputed to have been a pupil of Gandon, was an Irish painter and architect, and a leading designer of churches during the first half of the nineteenth century. It is no surprise, therefore, that the architecture of the Custom House is truly represented in his painting of the south and east facades and Custom House Quay (ill. 21).

Unlike Malton (cf. ill. 9), Byrne makes it clear that only the main facade is of Portland stone. Shown in this painting, also,

and not in Malton's, are the carved chimney urns and the plethora of chimney stacks.

The east elevation is as Gandon left it. Not only is it without the dormer storey (which was added much later), but the arcade itself is still open. Originally all four seven-bay arcades in the Custom House (the two on either side of the main south

21 Patrick Byrne, *The Custom House*, 1818

32

portico, and those in the east and west facades) were open. With time all except one, that in the riverside facade furthest from us in Byrne's picture, were glazed in, and it was only during the 1920s post-fire restoration that the other riverside arcade was opened again. The other two have remained closed.

In the bottom right-hand corner of this painting a sailing ship can just be seen, which is moored in the Custom House Dock, which ran parallel to the east side of the Custom House and was completed in 1796, later to be followed by two others, George's Dock and the Inner Dock (see ill. 58).

The choice of illustrations for this book has been an individual one, which has made possible the inclusion of J. Brandard's early nineteenth-century lithograph (ill. 22), which many purists would have excluded. The composition is poor, with little to link its three separate themes – a lively foreground scene, the Custom House and Quay with sailing ships alongside, and a wide expanse of sky and river.

So why, after such a doubtful introduction, was this print chosen? For a start, it is possible to appreciate the warm sunset colours in sky and water, even while noting that the over-large sun appears to be sinking behind a strange grey atmospheric band which conveniently screens Carlisle Bridge and beyond. The little cameo scene in the foreground, which has a cartoon element about it, repays scrutiny, with its still-life of barrels, basket and rough cart in the corner, rustic, pipe-smoking man, in his crumpled white stockings, sitting next to a Little Red Riding Hood figure and their three fat pigs. Alongside them a reluctant horse digs its hoofs in, in spite of the efforts of its riders and the bare-footed urchin tugging at its reins.

The main reason, however, for including this print is to point out just a few of the the many inaccuracies in the depic-

22 J. Brandard, *Custom House Quay*, an early 19th-century lithograph

23 J.G. Mulvaney (?), *The Custom House*, c.1830

lion and unicorn, and the pediment and frieze are minus their carving.

In spite of all this, and more which could be written (how correctly represented, for instance, are the sailing ships; and is the building at the far end of the quay supposed to be Northumberland Building, which was built on the corner of Eden Quay and Beresford Place between 1820 and 1830?), the print, perhaps for all the wrong reasons, was too interesting to exclude.

A mystery surrounds the painting shown in illustration 23 because, literally, it only came to light in 1969–70. It was found leaning against the wall in an attic in the old Ballast Office overlooking O'Connell Bridge, its frame damaged and its glass broken. In 1972 it was reglazed for an exhibition put on by the Dublin Port and Docks Board and thereafter hung in several offices until it finally came to rest in a large reception/committee room in the Port and Docks headquarters in Alexandra Road. In the early 1990s it was cleaned and re-canvassed, and its frame (probably the original) repaired, the expert who carried out this work tentatively dating it to around 1830 and attributing it to John George Mulvany (c.1766-1838). Mulvany, who was chosen as one of the original Members of the Royal Hibernian Academy in 1823, to which he regularly contributed, produced mainly landscape paintings, with occasional subject pieces.

If Mulvany was responsible for this picture, then it is obvious that architecture was not his strong point, as the Custom House is totally out of proportion; how tall and thin it looks, for instance, compared with Patrick Byrne's. Nevertheless, this is an attractive composition with much to commend it, which repays a closer look.

The artist has a lively interest in people and depicts them disporting themselves around the swing bridge; two bare-footed youths rest beside a bollard, one leaning against it and the

tion of the Custom House, so different to Patrick Byrne's. First of all, in order to squash as much of the Custom House as possible into his picture, the artist has concertinaed the facade, reducing the number of bays and packing the columns together. There would seem to be little chance of squeezing between the columns of the main portico, and none whatsoever between those in the two pavilion wings and the bays on either side of the main portico, where the columns have been pushed together to resemble, rather, a pilaster laid flat against the wall. Not only this, but he shows Corinthian rather than Doric capitals adorning the tops of the columns. Moving upwards to the coats of arms over the end pavilions, scrolls take the place of Smyth's

24 James Hore, *The Custom House (1)*, 1837

other, with a hole in the knee of his trousers, lying on the ground, the two of them presided over by a black-clad woman; a man, who seems to be wearing an over-abundance of coats, stands with his dog, looking down on two men seated below the bridge, one of whom is dangling his feet in the water, and a boy hangs at a dangerous angle over the railings of the bridge, wielding a long pole, for what purpose we do not know.

Although the river teems with sailing ships, and one paddle steamer churns up the water beside the quay, the main interest on the water is again concerned with people; a couple relax in a small sailing boat, one trailing a hand in the water, a passen-ger has just disembarked from a rowing boat at the quay steps, while a mid-river boat-load of passengers includes another Little Red Riding Hood figure (cf. ill. 22), who for some reason has chosen to travel standing up.

While the river is dark, reflecting the clouds overhead, the sun escapes to light up the Custom House and account for the people basking on the quayside, and the open window in the east pavilion of the Custom House suggests the heat of the day.

Many pictures in this book concentrate on the commercial side of things, but we have this artist to thank for a glimpse of the lighter side of life on Custom House Quay.

James Hore's treatment of light in the painting shown in illustration 24 gives it a luminous quality and yet, at the same time, it is meticulously drawn. The Custom House gleams white in the sunlight, so emphasising its luxurious Portland stone facade, which contrasts with the convincing red brick over stone terrace of houses in Beresford Place adjacent to it, long since demolished. Half hidden by masts, to the left of the painting, on the corner of Eden Quay and Beresford Place, is a building known to be the Northumberland Commercial and Family Hotel, or Northumberland Buildings (ill. 59), later to become Liberty Hall. From what can be made out between the masts, the representation does not seem to be an architecturally accurate one, unlike that of the Custom House where, although also partly obscured by rigging, even the niches, which alternated with the windows above the front seven-bay arcades before the 1921 fire, can be seen.

The rigging of the sailing ships, whose bows are moored to George's Quay (lack of space made it impossible for ships to lie alongside) is drawn with scrupulous attention to detail and Hore's introduction of bright colours into the headgear and clothing of some of his clusters of variously occupied people, and into the paintwork of the boats, makes a lively and animated contrast to the calm, majestic backdrop of the Custom House.

Nothing is known at present about James Hore's education or training, but he was almost certainly the second son of of Walter Hore of Seafield, County Wexford. He is known to have been in Rome in 1829, possibly on a Grand Tour, and three of his paintings, of which this is one (the other two being *The Four Courts* and *Trinity College and the Bank*) were shown at the Royal Academy in 1837.

Dr Michael Wynne, in the Spring 1985 issue of the *Irish Arts Review*, heads his contribution 'James Hore, Gentleman View-Painter', and this painting exemplifies the artist's right to that title, as does his other known painting of the Custom House (ill. 25).

At the Adam Salesrooms auction of July 1981, the painting shown in illustration 25, *A View of the Custom House, Dublin*, was catalogued as being by William Sadler. It bore no means of identification but, fortunately, the Directors of the Cynthia O'Connor Gallery realized from its stylistic mannerisms that it must be a James Hore. They were successful in bidding for it and, soon afterwards, sold it to a client, who has kindly allowed its reproduction here.

The painting's viewpoint is from Burgh Quay, at the junction with Hawkins Street, slightly further upriver than the Brocas engraving (ill. 64), which is similar to it in many respects. The building on the corner of Hawkins Street is still there, now a travel agency but then the premises of T.P. Wilson & Co., Seed Merchants, whose sign can be seen in the picture beside the first floor window. The jutting cornice of the Corn Exchange is outlined against the sky further down the quay.

Of the three buildings depicted on the opposite side of the river, only the Custom House has survived. Northumberland Buildings, on the corner of Eden Quay and Beresford Place, was just glimpsed through the ships' rigging in Hore's *Custom House* painting already discussed (ill. 24), but here it is very plain to see. The terrace beside it, three red-brick residential storeys above a stone shopping colonnade, demonstrates not only the symmetry beloved by the Wide Street Commissioners (who were responsible for planning the Dublin of the late eighteenth and early nineteenth century) but also, in regard to the shops beneath respectable residential quarters, their innovative borrowing from the Continent. As in the last painting, the wide sky, cloudy but bright, is pierced by ships' masts, and human activity abounds on both river and quayside.

James Hore's careful attention to architectural detail and his ability to capture on canvas the very texture of the building

25 (facing page) James Hore, *The Custom House (2)*, 1837

materials he portrays is notable. It is to be hoped that more of his works will emerge from obscurity in the future.

The topographical view of the Custom House from the River Liffey (shown in illustration 26) was one of a series of twelve Views of Dublin published by J. Le Petit, 20 Capel Street, in the 1820s, all of which were drawn by Samuel Frederick Brocas (c.1792-1847) and engraved by his younger brother Henry (c.1790-1846). Another of the twelve views, of the Corn Exchange, can be seen in illustration 64.

The drawing of the Custom House is reasonably accurate, with one glaring exception. The three niches which alternated with the windows on the first floor facade, above the two seven bay arcades, before the 1921 fire, have already been mentioned. Here, however, something has gone badly wrong, as *eight* bays are depicted. Did the artist realise his mistake? It would seem that he possibly did, because, in the east wing he has managed to mask the sixth bay from the left with the paddle steamer's funnel, so keeping the sequence of window, niche, window, etc. correct; the west wing mistake is similarly masked, this time with the sailing ship's rigging. One possible minor mistake is that the artist seems to have taken it upon himself to pop a lid on top of Edward Smyth's soup tureen urn, or is this just an inaccurate drawing of the urn with another little chimney pot sticking up out of it?

The entrance to the dock can be seen on the extreme right where, of course, a lock would have been in operation, as also at the entrance to George's Dock, further downstream. As in Mulvaney's painting (ill. 23), the iron railings separating the Old Dock Quay from the Custom House Quay are depicted, but this time a soldier is shown guarding the entrance.

By the 1820s, with the advent of the steam engine for ship propulsion, paddle steamers such as the one in the picture, would have been a common sight on the river. In addition to their steam propulsion they were also rigged for sails.

Thomas Sautell Roberts' *Dublin taken near the Custom House* (ill. 27) is inscribed: 'Dedicated to the Right Honble. the Commissioners of His Majesty's Revenue & Excise', which accounts for the emphasis placed on the Old Dock and shipping, and suggests that the Commissioners were the patrons for this work.

Sautell Roberts (1760-1826) took the name Thomas after the early death of his elder brother, Thomas, a talented painter, whose landscapes have been described as 'some of the most nostalgic and evocative ever painted of the country'. Sautell did not, at first, set out to follow in his brother's footsteps but intended to become an architect, like his father, 'Honest' John Roberts of Waterford. He attended the Dublin Society Architecture Schools, where he was apprenticed to Thomas Ivory, but architecture was not to his taste and he extricated himself as soon as possible, taking on not only his brother's name, but his artistic career, and completing some of his unfinished works.

Perhaps Thomas Sautell's brief introduction to architecture helped him in his portrayal of buildings. Although the drum of the Custom House dome in this instance is rather strange, looking more like a colonnaded walkway, on the whole the building is adequately represented. It becomes obvious when looking more closely at the picture, however, that the cityscape of red-brick buildings in the background is not authentic, except for a few recognisable spires and domes; for instance, the building squashed up against the north-east pavilion of the Custom House is straight out of Thomas' imagination. There certainly were warehouses in the vicinity of the Old Dock, but nothing has ever been that close to the Custom House.

But all this does not matter in the least because this lovely airy picture is about wide skies and a wide river, populated by ships looking beautiful under full sail. The fact that manoeuvrability

26 S.F. Brocas, *View of the Custom House from the River Liffey,* 1828

27 Thomas Sautell Roberts, *Dublin taken near the Custom House*, 1817

under full sail this high up the river was difficult to achieve does not seem to matter either. Although the river is crowded with vessels of one kind or another, the effect is strangely still and Coleridge's lines 'as idle as a painted ship upon a painted ocean' spring to mind. It is as if the river is of tinted glass, the foreground blue merging into delicate pink, which stretches back towards Carlisle Bridge and the Halfpenny Bridge beyond. The ships, mirrored in the glass, are arranged careful-

ly on it; no oars dip, no sails fill, and the little man in the front of the picture plane is left for ever teetering on the edge of his rowing boat.

The photograph reproduced in illustration 28 was published in Frederick H. Mares' *Photographs of Dublin*, in 1867, and clearly shows the swing bridge at the entrance to the Old Custom House Dock (see ill. 58), with a crane mounted on a pontoon

28 Fred H. Mares, A photograph published in 1867 showing the swing bridge at the entrance to the Custom House Dock

alongside it. A good idea can be gained from it, too, of the amount of shipping still using the Custom House Quay mid-way through the nineteenth century, which could still, at this time, proceed as far up the river as Carlisle Bridge.

There is an especially good view in this photograph of Northumberland Buildings, on the corner of Eden Quay and Beresford Place, behind the great pile of timber on the quay. Unusually, there is not a barrel in sight, but quayside clutter of one sort or another appears in all the early representations of

the Custom House. It was always a working area and only since 1978, with the Talbot Memorial Bridge (ill. 54) blocking access to it for all but the smallest vessels, has it assumed the appearance of an esplanade.

A comparison of this photograph with Patrick Byrne's painting (ill. 21) shows some interesting additions. As well as the iron railings already noted (supported by round-topped piers, which bear the familiar Gandonian patera and husk motif), a cluster of chimney pots now sprouts from the ornamental urn.

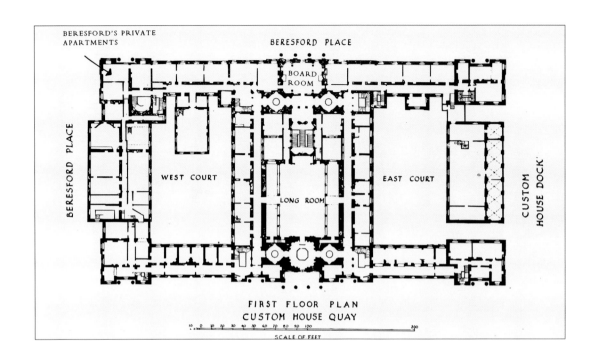

BERESFORD'S PRIVATE APARTMENTS

BERESFORD PLACE

BOARD ROOM

BERESFORD PLACE

WEST COURT

EAST COURT

LONG ROOM

CUSTOM HOUSE DOCK

FIRST FLOOR PLAN
CUSTOM HOUSE QUAY

SCALE OF FEET

FIRE, RECONSTRUCTION AND RESTORATION

On 25 May 1921, the Custom House was set on fire by the Dublin Brigade of the IRA. It burned for five days, at the end of which little was left of the original interior of the building. Had it not been for the wind direction at the time of the fire, the story could have been far worse. Because the wind was blowing from the south-east, it pushed the flames into the building, and away from the Portland stone facade; had this been damaged, it would have been irreplaceable.

Study of a Board of Works plan of the first floor, showing the building as it was before the fire (ill. 29), and an aerial photograph taken by the Army Air Corps after the fire (ill. 30), gives a good idea of the lay-out of the pre-fire interior. The centres of the long north and south facades were connected by one wide block, with a courtyard on either side. The major accommodation on the first floor of this central block comprised the Long Room and Board Room; John Beresford's private apart-

29 First floor plan prior to the 1921 fire

42

ments were in the western part of the main north-facing wing. The Long Room, which was the main space in the building where public business was transacted, was not really long at all, but nearly square, measuring 70' x 65', with a range of six Ionic columns along each side. A contributor to the *Irish Builder & Engineer* of 2 September 1916, writes of the Long Room: 'The space between the wall and columns is enclosed by a range of counters, behind which are placed the officers to transact the business. In this room forfeited goods are sold, and sales by inch of candle conducted'!

In the Board Room four fluted Corinthian columns proclaimed its status and, from its windows in the north portico, John Beresford could have looked directly across to Gandon's terrace of five houses in the street named after him, Beresford Place. His own sumptuously appointed private apartments were the cause of much contemporary hostility.

A reporter on the *Dublin Evening Post* of the late 1780s wrote of the fifty mahogany doors and a suite which would 'vie with oriental magnificence – with the palaces of Kings and Princes'.

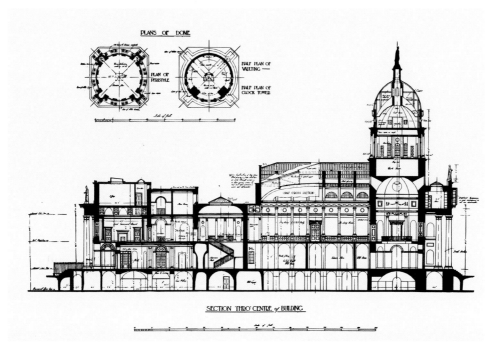

32 Section showing the building before the fire

Some time after the fire had died down a comprehensive photographic record of the fire damage was made. Illustration 31 shows the amputated columns and sorry remains of the Long Room, while illustration 33 would be funny if it was not so sad; the copper dome having melted completely away, it shows the statue of Commerce still intact on her plinth, but a plinth of which far more is seen than was originally intended. Although the drum and colonnade survived the fire, they were found to be too badly damaged for restoration and so were demolished to roof level and rebuilt, as has already been mentioned.

31 (facing page) The fire-damaged Long Room

Sutcliffe's section (ill. 32) shows the dome and Long Room as they were before the fire. From the ground floor vestibule beneath the dome it was possible to look up, through an oculus in the ceiling, to the domed ceiling of the floor above. The frieze encircling the drum of this first floor dome was embellished with Edward Smyth's fine stone relief sculpture, which could be seen through the oculus. Although Smyth's carving was undamaged by the fire, the oculus was closed during the 1920s restoration. Now, as part of the Custom House Visitor Centre, this oculus has been reopened and Smyth's carving can be enjoyed once more. It is easy to forget, when standing under the first floor dome, that, as Sutcliffe's section illustrates, the

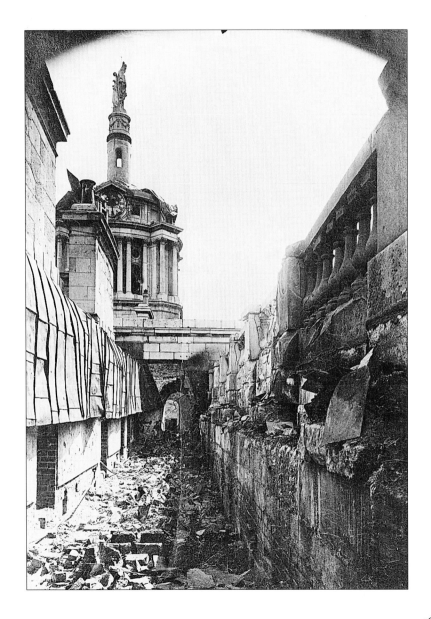

dome rises, unseen from inside, to the same height again.

In the photograph of the Custom House on fire (ill. 34) the chimney stacks and four portico statues (in a blackened state) are still in position but it is no longer possible to distinguish between what was window and what was niche in the row of burnt-out first-floor window frames.

A point to notice in this photograph is that the arcade on the east side of the portico was glazed some time before the 1921 fire. Perhaps the only good thing to come out of the fire was that this arcade was reopened during the restoration.

At Easter time, 1926, the following review of the film *Irish Destiny* appeared in the *Dublin Evening Mail* of Saturday, 10 April 1926: 'So insistent have been the demands for admission to the Corinthian Cinema during the week to see the now much talked of film "Irish Destiny", that the management have decided to continue the showing of this beautiful picture all next week. "Irish Destiny" – which features some of the most dramatic episodes of the historic Anglo-Irish struggle – was written and produced by Mr I. J. Eppel, MD, managing director of Eppels' Films Ltd. In its production Dr Eppel was assisted by men who actually took part in the thrilling and exciting incidents portrayed, and several of the players will be readily recognised. Amongst the scenes depicted are the burning of the Dublin Custom House, holds-up in the city, raids by Auxiliaries, and a big ambush. "Irish Destiny" contains the highest elements of art, action, scenery, and photography. It is a triumph for Irish enterprise.'

In the mid-1980s this film came to light again when two copies of the poster advertising it (ill. 35) were found under the lino of an old house in Dublin undergoing renovation. The posters, one measuring 5' x 6', the other almost six foot square,

33 The fire-damaged second-floor corridor with dome in background

34 The Custom House
on fire, May 1921

were fine examples of the off-set lithographic processes of the time. Generously donated to the Irish Film Archive, which now holds them, they were subjected to a full preservation process which involved de-acidifying, washing and repair.

The finding of the posters set in train a search for a print of the film, which was duly tracked down in the Library of Congress in Washington. On Saturday 11 December 1993, in the presence of Her Excellency, Mary Robinson, President of Ireland and Patron of the Film Institute of Ireland, in the National Concert Hall, the Irish Film Archive screened the film, with a new score of music by Mícheál Ó Súilleabháin.

The film combines the weaving of a romantic narrative with the use of actuality footage, with an all too fleeting glimpse of the Custom House on fire.

Eppel did not make another film, and *Irish Destiny* stands alone in Irish film-making of the 1920s in its treatment of the events of 1920-21.

Apart from some lobbies and vestibules, little remains of Gandon's original Custom House interior and no attempt was made by the Board of Works, in their 'restoration' programme of 1926-30, to reconstruct it as it had been. A comparison of the pre-and post-fire plans (ills. 29 & 37) and a study of the Air Corps' post-reconstruction aerial photograph of 1939 (ill. 36) show that the main alteration took place in the centre of the building. Where there was originally one centre block, connecting the north and south facades and containing the Long Room, there were now two, the outer walls of the two new blocks (facing the east and west courtyards) following the same line as the original centre block. Between the two blocks a light well was created, beneath which, in the basement, central heating boilers were installed. All chimneys, except the ornamental urns, were done away with, replaced by one single massive chimney stack on the main axis to the north of the light well.

The east and west courtyards were excavated to basement level and the two centre blocks reduced to one storey over basement, with a flat roof. In 1939-40 they were raised by one storey (which has not yet happened in illustration 36).

After the reconstruction Commerce was returned to her pedestal, but the four badly damaged statues from the front portico were removed, to face a long exile in the Custom House grounds, before they were reprieved in the late 1980s. The removal of glazing from the south-east arcade and the use of Ardbraccan limestone for the drum of the dome have already been mentioned.

The photograph in illustration 39 shows the two huge murals, designed by Robert Ballagh, which covered part of the south facade of the Custom House while the most recent restoration work was taking place. They were officially unveiled on 22 July 1988.

It occurred to David Slattery, the Office of Public Works architect in charge of the restoration programme, that, as hoarding would be necessary anyway, a virtue could be made of necessity, and so the idea of the mural took off. Robert Ballagh's design was adopted and Sisks, the contractors for the restoration work, provided the heavy framework and standard-size plywood panels, each measuring 8' x 6', necessary for the job.

Two problems remained. Gallons and gallons of paint would be required and, unless Robert Ballagh was to spend much of the rest of his life at the job, he would need assistants. A paint company immediately offered to sponsor the paint and it was arranged that eighteen unemployed young people, who were attending an art and design course run by the North City Community Action Project (funded by ANCO, which has since become FÁS), should be employed, under the eye of their tutor and Robert Ballagh, to carry out the work. This work was to

35 Poster advertising film,
Irish Destiny, 1926

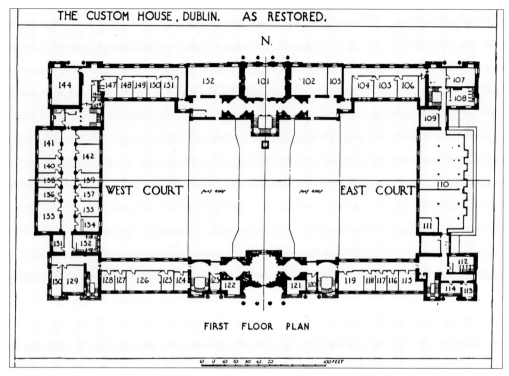

THE CUSTOM HOUSE, DUBLIN.   AS RESTORED.

N.

WEST COURT   EAST COURT

FIRST FLOOR PLAN

37 Plan of reconstructed building, 1930

constitute part of their course and each was to receive a certificate when it was completed, of which they might well be proud, for the mural was the largest ever to be painted in Ireland.

The problem of where to prepare the vast project was solved when the Custom House Docks Development Authority generously offered to make Stack A available, the huge warehouse which was one of the locations used in the recent Michael Collins film (see also page 57 below).

The work, which took two months to complete, was designed by Ballagh in such a way that the young people were able to carry it out entirely on their own. First of all the plywood strips were painted white. Then, the original drawing having been scaled right up, the team drew the architectural design on the panels in pencil. The next step was to carefully cover each pencil line with quarter-inch masking tape, paint over the whole lot with blue paint and then strip off the tape to

36 (facing page) Aerial view, c.1939, after the reconstruction

38 Cover of student magazine, 1988

When it was all over, Sisks threw a party for the young people who, in their turn, produced a humorous magazine recounting their experiences while involved with the 'Costom House Murial' (ill. 38).

In 1979 the detachment of a sizeable piece of stone from the Custom House signalled that all was not well with its structure, but it was not until 1986 that conservation and restoration work began. The contract was awarded to John Sisk & Co. and David Slattery was the Office of Public Works architect in charge of the project, assisted by Alistair Lindsay. The work was completed in May 1991, the year of the 200th anniversary of the Custom House, at a total cost of £6 million. Illustration 40 shows the building as it is to-day, fully restored, with the Portland stone facade gleaming after its cleaning.

When the work began, no measured drawings were available and so a full photogrammetric survey of the building (the first in Ireland) was carried out. It was necessary to locate the ferrous metal beneath the surface which, by its expansion due to corrosion, was damaging the surrounding stonework. Gandon had encased his metal cramps in lead but could not have foreseen that much of this would melt in the great heat of the 1921 fire. The problem of how to locate the metal was solved when David Slattery hit upon the bright idea of calling in the army bomb disposal squad. With their mine detectors they were able to pinpoint the location of the tons of hidden metal beneath the fabric, which could then be related to the drawings to show the pattern of decay. Ultrasonics were used to identify the cracks in the Portland stone columns, so enabling repair instead of replacement, as Slattery's policy was to save as much of the original stonework as possible. Only 10% of the original stone had to be replaced although, as was mentioned earlier, the story would have been very different but for the south-east wind which blew the flames of the 1921 fire into the building and away from the

expose the white design below. Finally the plywood strips were assembled onto the frame Sisks had made and small pieces of extra wood affixed to the top and side of the frame to accommodate the overlapping scroll, pencil, set square, etc. and achieve the desired *trompe l'oeil* effect. The names of all the people who had participated in the painting were recorded on the simulated label on the bottom right hand corner of the work covering the east pavilion.

39 Robert Ballagh's 1988 mural

Portland stone facade. The *Irish Times* of 11 May 1991 recorded Slattery as saying: 'Real conservation isn't about making old buildings look better for purely cosmetic reasons; it's about saving every fragment you can of the original building. It would be inexcusable to do otherwise.' It was necessary to replace the entire crowning balustrade with Portland stone, as cast concrete had been employed in the 1926 renovation. The string course (which runs round the building at the level of the keystones) and one complete and one partial portico attic storey were also replaced. Skilled masons worked on all the carved stonework, the four statues over the south portico, fully restored, taking their places again for the first time since the fire.

40 The building after the 1986-91 restoration   **41** (facing page) Aerial view of the Custom House and its environs, 1997

HISTORIC ASSOCIATIONS

The Custom House Docks, together with accompanying locks, warehouses and stores, were all part of Gandon's original brief (cf. ill. 58) and John Rennie (1761-1821) was appointed as consultant. What became known as the Old Dock was opened first, in 1796, followed by George's Dock (named after George IV) in 1821 and the Inner Dock some years later. The entrances to the Old Dock and George's Dock were through sea-locks. Until the 1840s most ships (including the early paddle steamers) were small enough to lock in and out of the docks, but this could only be done over a three-hour period at high water.

In 1845 negotiations were completed for the leasing of the Custom House Docks (excluding the warehouses, which were leased to the Scovell brothers for a term of 45 years from 1824) to the Ballast Board. The docks would remain the property of the Crown, who would receive a nominal rent of five shillings per annum. From October 1866, ownership of the Custom House Docks Complex was vested in the Dublin Port and Docks Board and, on expiration of the Scovell lease in 1869, the board took over the operation of the warehouses.

Business at the three Custom House Docks gradually declined. Proposed alterations were never implemented, as the potential for deepwater berthage further downstream grew, free from any hindrance of locks or tides. The Old Dock fell into disuse and, in 1927, was filled in, Memorial Road and the re-aligned western boundary of the docks complex now covering its site (ill. 41). The Matt Talbot Bridge, where it leaves Custom House Quay, lies over the site of the lock and entrance into the Old Dock. Until 1975 George's Dock and the Inner Dock were used as coal banks by the coal trade, but this stopped when a new bulk discharge facility was provided at South Bank Quay.

The potential of the area for redevelopment was recognized by the Government, who provided, in the Urban Renewal Act of 1986, for the establishment of the Custom House Docks Development Authority, with a brief to secure the redevelopment of the 27-acre Custom House Docks area, seven acres of which was composed of the two inter-linked dock basins. The Port & Docks Board moved its operations to sites in the port area, where its headquarters are now in Alexandra Road, just beyond the Point Depot.

As can be seen from the photograph shown in illustration 41, the development of the twenty-seven acres is now almost complete. Stack A (to the right of George's Dock) is to be conserved. The Reverend G.N. Wright wrote of this building, in 1821, that there was not one particle of wood or other combustible matter in it, that the roof was supported by metal framework of 'an ingenious construction', with long lanterns inserted, and that the entire framework was supported by three rows of cylindrical metal pillars, 26 in each row, resting on others of granite which continued through the stone floor into the vaults beneath.

The reason why Stack A was sometimes known as the 'Banquet Hall' will be recounted on the next page.

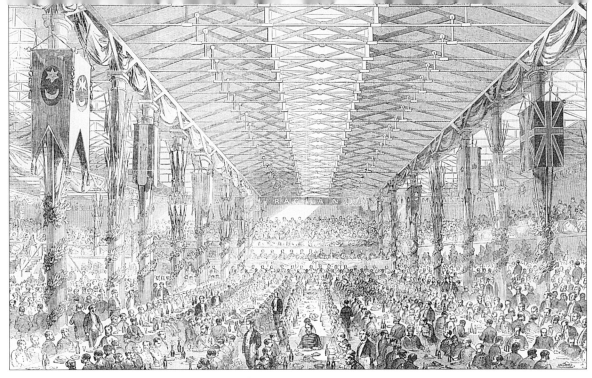

42 The great 'Crimean Banquet', 1856

In August 1856, the Lord Mayor of Dublin, Fergus Farrell, convened a meeting which unanimously proposed: 'That ... steps should be taken to give a National entertainment, in the City of Dublin, to the troops now stationed in this country, who have served in the Crimea.' So began the weeks of planning which were to culminate in the great Crimean Banquet (ill. 42). A subscription list was opened and, by 19 September, £2000 had already been collected. As it was anticipated that 4000 people would sit down to eat, and another 1000 spectators would enjoy the occasion, a sufficiently large venue had to be sought. An offer from Mr Henry Scovell, which suggested using his great bonded warehouse (now known as Stack A), solved the problem, especially when Mr Gardner, the Collector of Customs, volunteered to be responsible for clearing the bonded goods from the warehouse for the occasion.

The great day dawned and the 3,628 invited guests converged upon the Custom House Docks, free rail transport having been provided for those coming from a distance. One thousand five hundred military guests came from the regiments stationed in Dublin, 1,000 from the Curragh and the remainder from various stations throughout the country. There were also 500 pensioners, constabulary, police and marines.

The warehouse was transformed for the occasion, the iron framework supporting the roof being painted in red, cobalt blue and yellow, the pillars a deep blue and the walls of the building white. Flags of every nation abounded and emotive names of bat-

43 The launch of *The City of Dublin* lifeboat, 1867

tles and heroes (and heroines – Florence Nightingale was not forgotten) were inscribed in large letters on the walls.

With the exception of hot potatoes and plum puddings, the meal was cold, and the statement of the viands supplied by Messrs Spadacini & Murphy reads:'250 hams, 230 legs of mutton, 500 meat pies, 100 venison pasties, 100 rice puddings, 260 plum puddings, 200 turkeys, 200 geese, 250 pieces of beef, weighing in all upwards of 3,000 lbs, three tons of potatoes, 2,000 two lb. loaves, 100 capons and chickens and 6 ox tongues'. Newspapers the next day reported that 'much merriment was caused among the crowd, by the arrival of the potatoes, in four vans, which hove in sight steaming like locomotives. One of the vans, resembling the machines used for the removal of furniture, was drawn by two horses, and the driver was literally enveloped in clouds of steam.' Local merchants contributed to the occasion. Mr Henry Brennan, wine merchant, supplied 'a sufficient quantity of port or sherry wine to afford each soldier invited one pint'; Mr Martin, timber merchant, lent sufficient timber for tables and forms; and Messrs Todd, Burns & Co., of Henry Street, provided all the cloths used for the tables, galleries, banners, etc. free of charge. The cloth on the Lord Lieutenant's table alone was of fine linen damask, six feet wide and 84 feet long, in one piece.

The Custom House Dock Quay and the Old Dock Quay were the scene of arrivals and departures other than those concerned with imports and exports. The picture in illustration 43 appeared in the *Illustrated London News* of 16 February 1867, and concerns the launching of a lifeboat; but before telling the story there are points of interest to be noticed about the Custom House. The east elevation is depicted, showing the north-east pavilion and part of the seven-bay arcade. The artist has omitted the riverine head from above the pavilion door, and has put his own pattern into the tympanum (compare with ill. 44),

44 North-east pavilion
of Custom House

instead of Gandon's familiar patera and husk motif; he has also given the chimney urn flutes which it never had and changed the fenestration of the pavilion. The high roof of the Long Room can be seen rising above the roof of the arcade, where the bays have, by now been filled in (if the artist has got it right).

The scene represented is the launching of *The City of Dublin*, from the Old Custom House Dock. The boat was presented to the Royal National Lifeboat Institution by the citizens of Dublin and was to be stationed at Courtmacsherry, Co. Cork.

Many dignatories attended the launch and the Duchess of Abercorn, wife of the Lord Lieutenant, performed the usual ceremony of breaking a bottle of sherry against the prow. The boat, together with her crew, had journeyed to the dockside on a wagon drawn by eight horses, as part of a procession from the Mansion House which included the Lord Mayor, in his state coach, Aldermen and other members and officers of the Corporation, a number of seamen and the band of the Scots

Greys. The whole event took place in pouring rain, from which there was no covered space on the quayside for those engaged in the ceremony or for the crowds of spectators.

A statement of subscription and address of thanks were read out and, after cheers all round, the lifeboat was ready for launching. The boat was 32' long and 7½' wide, with accommodation for ten oarsmen, 'double banked', and was launched by a most ingenious contrivance, whereby it was 'sprung' directly from the carriage into the dock, with all hands on board. The idea of this was that, in a sea launch, the crew, oars in hand, would be enabled to obtain headway before the breakers had time to beat the boat broadside to the beach.

The gift of this boat brought the total of lifeboats stationed around the Irish coast to 172, all under the management of the Royal National Lifeboat Institution.

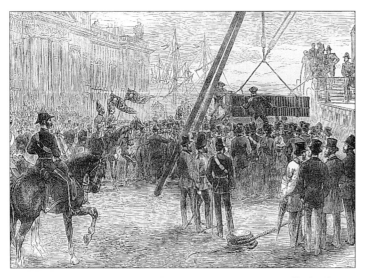

45 The funeral of the Viceroy of India, 1872 : Lord Mayo's coffin landing at the Custom House Quay

Richard Southwell Bourke, sixth Earl of Mayo (1822-72), succeeded to the Irish earldom on the death of his father in 1867. As Lord Naas he served three terms as Chief Secretary and at the end of his final term, in 1868, was appointed Viceroy and Governor-General of India. On 8 February 1872, en route to Calcutta from Burma in the man-of-war *Glasgow*, he broke his voyage at the Andaman Islands, in the Bay of Bengal, to visit the penal colony there. It was night as he returned to his ship after the inspection and, before his guards realized what was happening, his convict assassin had leapt from the dark and stabbed him twice in the back.

The *Illustrated London News* reported the slow progress of Lord Mayo's body back to Ireland by sea. It arrived in Calcutta on 17 February, where it lay in state in the Throne Room for three days before continuing on to Bombay and then, via Suez, home. It reached Dublin Bay late in the evening of Wednesday, 24 April 1872, and the next day the Admiralty yacht *Enchantress* landed the remains of 'this lamented nobleman' on the Custom House Quay at twelve noon (ill. 45). The coffin, presumably of lead, was, as the newspaper reports, of great weight (which, without disrespect, was perhaps just as well, considering the time its journey had taken) and was lowered to the quayside by machinery.

The Lord Lieutenant of Ireland, Earl Spencer, took the leading part in the 'mournful ceremony', coming from the Castle on horseback, escorted by King's Dragoon Guards. Accompanied by a long procession the coffin, on a gun-carriage, proceeded over Carlisle Bridge, by Westmoreland Street, College Green, Dame Street, Parliament Street, Essex Bridge, the Four Courts, and then up the north quays. The entire route was lined by military personnel and the effect heightened 'by the music of 160 instruments in perfect accord'.

The procession then broke up and the funeral proceeded to Naas, reaching Palmerstown House that evening before dark. The interment took place on the following day, in the Johnstown Cemetery.

46   Rose Barton, *Departure of the 4th Dragoon Guards from Dublin*, 1891

Rose Barton's McCalmont half-brothers lived at Mount Juliet, Co. Kilkenny, and one of them, General Sir Hugh McCalmont, was in command of the 4th Dragoon Guards. Rose's painting of *The Departure of the 4th Dragoon Guards from Dublin, June 18, 1891* (ill. 46), stayed in the family until November 1993, when it was sold at Sotheby's to a private collector.

A trawl through the contemporary newspapers revealed no report of the regiment's departure and the only mention found was in *The Times* of 18 June 1891, which reported that the '4th Dragoon Guards, about to arrive from Dublin at Aldershot, are for India (Bengal Presidency) in 1892'. This was better than nothing, as it confirmed that Rose was, indeed, recording an actual military event.

The composition falls into two parts, one concerned with people and buildings and the other with ships and water. The Custom House, depicted in soft mauvish hues, provides a backdrop to the sharply delineated, vividly uniformed, departing soldiers, their horses, and the little crowd of onlookers. The sun, which from the length of the shadows, would seem to be low in the sky, brightens even more the soldiers' jackets and shining helmets, and highlights the smooth rumps of the horses, and the dress of the one, solitary, pink-clad female. With an expanse of quay in the foreground, and the characters set well back into the picture plane, the effect of recession is enhanced.

The part of the painting concerned with ships and water presents an atmospheric mood, entirely different to the vibrant one upon the quay. Although the two ships berthed against the Custom House Quay are sharply drawn, the masts of those moored on the other side of the river merge into the smoky, misty haze which obscures the middle distance.

Born in Ireland in 1856, Rose showed early artistic talent. With her friend Mildred Anne Butler, she studied in Paris under the popular salon painter Henri Gervex. Although she was to paint throughout the rest of her life, she was not admit-

and the Funeral of Lord Mayo – were specific events, but Guinness' association with the Quay has been constant down through the years. Until the Talbot Memorial Bridge was built in 1978, so cutting off access, Guinness boats moored at the Custom House Quay were a common sight. In the photograph shown in illustration 47, taken in the early 1950s, Joachim Gerstenberg has combined Guinness boats with the dignified backdrop of the Custom House to make a most effective composition.

In the left foreground is the *Sandyford*, one of a fleet of Guinness barges which, in convoys of three, plied up and down the river between the brewery wharf at Victoria Quay and Custom House Quay, delivering full casks of stout to be loaded onto the seagoing fleet, and collecting the empties. Painted in the company's blue and cream livery, with red and black funnels, each had a skipper, a mate, three bargemen and an engine driver. All the barges were equipped with hinged funnels, which were lowered when passing under the bridges. It was the practice of small city boys, leaning over the parapets, to shout down to the bargemen: 'Hey, mister! Bring us back a parrot'! In June, 1961, the barges were withdrawn from service, the short journey between brewery and port being taken by road.

The larger ship in this photograph, moored beside the Custom House Quay, is the *Clarecastle*, built in 1914 by Scott and Sons of Bowling, on the Clyde; until 1952 she, the *Carrowdore* and the *Guinness* maintained the company's export trade to Britain (the *Guinness* having replaced the *Clareisland* in 1931). They all came through the Second World War relatively unscathed, although in 1941 the *Carrowdore* had a narrow escape when she was attacked by a German bomber fifteen miles off the Irish coast and a bomb ricochetted off the forecastle into the sea before exploding; the fin of the bomb was caught in the deck fittings and can be seen in the Guinness Hop Store Museum.

47 Guinness boats at Custom House Quay, *c.1950*

ted to full membership of the Royal Watercolour Society until 1911. She divided her time between London and Dublin, but finally she settled in Knightsbridge, where she died on 11 October 1929.

The stories relating to the Custom House Quay told so far – the Departure of the 4th Dragoons, the Launching of the Lifeboat

LIFFEY BRIDGES

If the question were asked which idea came first, to build a new Custom House or a new bridge over the Liffey, nearer the sea and the new city centre than Essex Bridge, the answer would probably be a new bridge. Why, then, was the Custom House built first (completed in 1791) and the bridge second (completed and opened to carriage traffic in 1795)? The answer to this would probably be because of the clever machinations of those with a vested interest in moving the city's centre eastwards; the likes, for instance, of Revenue Commissioner Luke Gardiner, whose prestigious residential developments north of the river were rapidly extending to the east. Such continued development depended on the building of a new bridge, to link the fashionable residential areas on the north with the centres of academic, parliamentary and social life on the south. If a new bridge was built, then a new Custom House would have to be built as well, downstream, as the old one would no longer be accessible to tall-masted ships. So, putting the cart before the horse, the Revenue Commissioners made out a case for a new site for the Custom House to the Lord Lieutenant, pointing out that the growth of the east end of town called for a new bridge to the east of Capel Street (and hence a new Custom House), and anyway the then Custom House site was far too restricted, making it necessary for ships of deep draught to offload their cargoes further downstream. With a new Custom House this

48 (above) An early print of Carlisle (now O'Connell) Bridge

49 Shipping at Burgh Quay and Eden Quay, *c.*1870, with Carlisle Bridge in the foreground

50 The original Butt (swivel) Bridge, showing the view of the Custom House from Burgh Quay prior to 1891

would be avoided and there would be a greater security in the collection of duties.

The rest of the story is history. Gandon's Custom House was built first, followed by his Carlisle Bridge (now O'Connell Bridge). Originally with an obelisk at each corner (ill. 48), which were removed in the early nineteenth century, the bridge was considerably narrower than the avenues built to approach it, and was rebuilt in its present form, to a design by Bindon Stoney, the Port and Docks Board Engineer, opening to traffic in 1880. The finished bridge was the same width as the adjoining Sackville (now O'Connell) Street, and was renamed after Daniel O'Connell. Keystones, in the style of Edward Smyth, were inserted in each central arch elevation, and the original ones can still be seen on the side of a red-brick building on Sir John Rogerson's Quay.

Carlisle Bridge thus became, in 1795, the last Liffey bridge before the sea. How narrow it was, and how high its balustrades,

can be seen in illustration 49 (a photograph taken from the corner of Lower O'Connell Street and Bachelor's Walk), with sailing ships now moored right up close to it, on Burgh Quay and Eden Quay.

The photograph at the top of this page shows the view of the Custom House which could be enjoyed from Burgh Quay before the Loopline railway bridge was built in 1891. In the foreground is the precursor to to-day's Butt Bridge, which was commonly known as the Swivel Bridge and connected Beresford Place on the north to Tara Street on the south. It was opened in 1879. Before discussing it, a further look should be taken at the Custom House behind it.

Even without the clue of the swivel bridge, this is recognisable as an early, pre-fire picture because the roofline still has its full complement of statues and chimneys; we can make out the niches which alternate with the first floor windows over the front arcades; the drum supporting the dome has not yet been rebuilt

51 View looking west along Eden Quay, showing the original Butt Bridge, *c*.1880

in Ardbraccan limestone; and, to the right of the photograph, we can see from the ships' masts that the Old Custom House Dock is still in use. It is of interest, too, that the arcade on the west facade of the Custom House has already been closed, and has remained so to this day. To the left of the bridge, at the junction of Beresford Place with Custom House Quay, can be seen Deane & Woodward's obelisk-like drinking fountain, erected *c*.1861.

In 1876, at the same time as a parliamentary act provided for the widening and improvement of Carlisle Bridge, permission was granted for the construction of a swivel bridge further downstream, to the west of the Custom House, which would open to allow shipping to continue to sail through to lie at Burgh Quay and Eden Quay. Binden Stoney also designed this four-span bridge, which would comprise a fixed masonry arch at either end and a central metal span which could rotate horizontally on a central pier, so opening a navigation channel on either side. With the building of the Loopline railway bridge in 1891, it was no longer possible for any but the smallest vessels to proceed up-river and on 13 December 1888 the bridge was closed for the last time.

The photograph shown in illustration 51 must have been taken around the time of the one on the previous page because, again, we can see the swivel bridge (1879) before the advent of the Loopline (1891). It was probably taken from the Custom House roof and this time looks upriver. There is more going on here than in the last photograph, with a number of ships moored in the stretch of water between the two bridges. Records show that the number of times the swivel bridge was opened in a year became less and less – 324 times in 1880 and, by 1888, only 27 – which suggests that this photograph, with its busier shipping activity, may be an earlier one.

Once more, on the corner of Beresford Place and Eden Quay, we see, more clearly than previously, the south elevation of Northumberland Buildings. It will be more than twenty years before the shelling of 1916 reduces it to the sorry state we see in illustration 59.

The purpose of the heap of coal on the quayside is unclear. It could be for fuelling steamships, or it could have been dumped by a collier for collection and distribution around the city. The little drays, loaded with full sacks, to be seen near the heap, would suggest the latter.

Illustration 52 is a photograph taken *c.*1891, shortly after the Loopline Bridge was built to carry the railway across the river, from a point near the corner of Bachelors Walk and Lower O'Connell Street. (It will be noted, comparing this photograph with illustration 49, that O'Connell Bridge has by now been widened; unfortunately, space does not permit discussion of the

52 O'Connell Bridge with the old Butt Bridge and the new Loopline Bridge in the background, *c.*1891

53 The new Butt Bridge (opened in 1932) and the Loopline : a recent photograph

interesting activity going on all around it – the horse-drawn tram, for instance, with the person sitting on the top deck under an umbrella!). The swivel bridge has not yet been replaced by the new Butt Bridge, but the vista formed by Gandon's beautiful building from this point, and any other west of the Loopline, has been lost for ever, as the ugly metal bridge slashes across its south and west facades.

In 1932 the Butt Bridge we know to-day opened to traffic, replacing Bindon Stoney's swivel bridge. It was designed by Joseph Mallagh and was the first Liffey bridge in Dublin to be built with reinforced concrete. While construction was in progress pedestrians could still cross the river at this point by a footbridge spanning the supports of the adjacent Loopline Bridge. The present Butt Bridge can be seen in a photograph (ill. 53) taken, as we can see by the statues, after the most recent restoration of the Custom House had been completed, from a viewpoint similar to that in illustration 50. What a difference! Now, bisected by the Loopline, with its obtrusive advertising, and engulfed by new buildings, from this point the Custom House is virtually lost to us. One of the very best views of it, however, although fleeting, can be seen from a train crossing the Loopline Bridge!

The Loopline was built amidst widespread opposition because it would obstruct the view of the Custom House. James Larkin, in 1939, commented that 'the Loopline was the foulest thing that ever disgraced the city'. For those with sharp eyes, a tiny concession to the Custom House has been made on one of the columns supporting the Loopline bridge; round the necking are alternated not harps and roses, but harps and shamrocks!

In 1991 the Office of Public Works commissioned a set of 25 drawings from James Horan to depict the city of Dublin as it appears at the end of the twentieth century, and to celebrate Dublin's role as the European City of Culture in that year. So began three years of work for James Horan, which culminated in the publication of *25 Views of Dublin*, in 1994.

His meticulous drawing of the Custom House (ill. 54) was made in April 1991 and was one of the first he undertook. It coincided with the completion of David Slattery's restoration programme. Since this drawing was made the skyline has changed, with the removal of the gasometer.

The Talbot Memorial Bridge, which can be seen here spanning the river to the east of the Custom House, was opened for traffic in February 1978, and was the first Liffey bridge in Dublin to use prestressed concrete as a structural medium. Its building was necessitated by the inability of Butt Bridge to cope with increased traffic demands.

With Butt Bridge becoming a one-way northbound crossing, and the new bridge a one-way southbound crossing (a situation which still obtains to-day) traffic congestion was considerably eased.

The Talbot Memorial Bridge connects Memorial Road, on the north side, to Moss Street on the south side. In 1952 Memorial Road had been formed by extending Beresford Place to curve around the north side of the Custom House down to meet Custom House Quay, and by a branch northwards to meet the junction of Store Street and Amiens Street (see ill. 41). As has been mentioned already, both Memorial Road and the foundations for the north side of Talbot Memorial Bridge lie over the original Custom House Dock, filled in in 1927.

With the advent of the new bridge it was no longer possible for larger shipping to berth at Custom House Quay or George's Quay, and City Quay became the furthest point upstream which they could reach. In 1984 the East Link Toll Bridge opened but, as it has a lifting span, shipping can still get as far upriver as Talbot Bridge (see modern map: ill. 78).

54 (facing page) James Horan, *The Custom House*, 1991

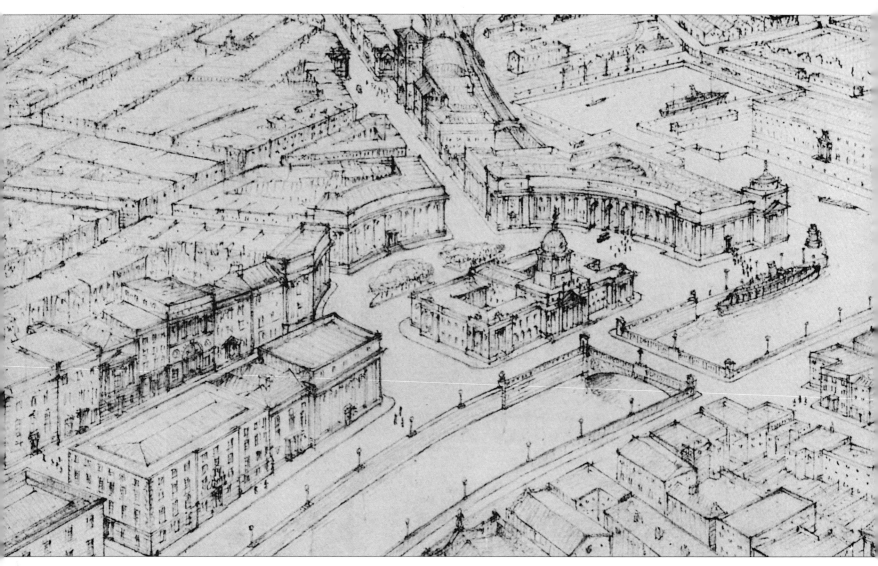

55 A townplanner's sketch for the 'Custom House Crescent', 1916

THE ENVIRONS OF THE CUSTOM HOUSE

In 1914 the Civics Institute of Ireland promoted an international competition aimed at securing plans and reports for the development of the City of Dublin, with special proposals for meeting the housing needs of the population. In 1916 first prize was awarded to Patrick Abercrombie and Sydney and Arthur Kelly, and in 1922 their scheme was published in a book entitled *Dublin of the Future*. The caption to their sketch showing plans for the Custom House surrounds (ill. 55) reads: 'CUSTOM HOUSE CRESCENT AND RIVERSIDE STATION. This sketch shows the Railway across the Liffey taken underground; the Butt Bridge removed; a new road Bridge facing the Custom House; the Riverside Station on the site of the old Dock and the Docks remodelled for the passenger steamers; the Crescent completed; and the approach to Amiens Street Station improved.'

Beresford Place, its arc completed and renamed Custom House Crescent, has a feeling of St Peter's Square, Rome, about it, with its pillared colonnade. Gardiner Street and the re-aligned Amiens Street enter the Crescent at an angle, on either side of a new central block (to replace Gandon's terrace), facing the main north entrance to the Custom House.

The sketch shows that long before it actually happened, in 1927, plans were afoot to fill in the Old Dock. Like to-day's Custom House Docks Development Authority, these early planners wished to retain George's Dock and the Inner Dock, but, in their case, not as an amenity area but as an arrival and departure zone for passenger steamers, with an attractive riverside station to serve both rail and sea travellers.

56 Harry Clarke, *The Last Hour of the Night*, 1922

57 James Gandon, *Elevation of Beresford Place*, 1790

The winning Abercrombie plan was never put into operation. When the competition was first mooted the Post Office, Custom House and Four Courts were all more or less in their original state. By the time the winning plan was published in 1922, all three had become fire-damaged victims of the country's political upheaval, as is illustrated by Harry Clarke in his telling frontispiece to the 1922 book (ill. 56), which also affirms that the planners' resolve to bring about 'the total abolition of slum conditions' had then come to naught.

A comparison between illustration 41 (a recent aerial photograph of the Custom House and area surrounding it), and illustration 58 (Taylor's 1824 plan) shows almost better than words the changes which have taken place in Beresford place in the last 200 years.

In 1757 an Act was passed 'for making a wide and convenient Way, Street, or Passage from Essex Bridge to the Castle of Dublin' and the Commissioners appointed to effect this work, and the subsequent development of the whole city of Dublin, became known as the Wide Streets Commissioners.

In 1790, plans were approved for the realignment of streets in the immediate environs of the Custom House, and Gardiner Street, Store Street, and Beresford Place came into being, and Abbey Street was connected to Beresford Place. On 26 November 1790, the Commissioners approved Gandon's elevation for the crescent of buildings facing the north of the Custom House (ill. 57), which was to be entirely residential in deference to the palatial northern facade of the Custom House opposite it. All this happened just in time because, after the Act of Union in 1800, no new schemes of any magnitude were initiated.

Taylor's plan shows that, at this time, Beresford Place ended abruptly at the iron railings which surrounded the Old Dock on its west and south sides. The Old Dock was filled in in 1927

As recently as 1993, a competition was held for the design of a *replacement* Loopline Bridge over the Liffey, but Abercrombie and his partners planned to do away with it altogether, taking the trains under the river instead. The idea of replacing Butt Bridge with one centred on the main Custom House facade was an attractive one and would have provided, for the first time, a head-on vista of Gandon's beautiful building as it was approached down a wide avenue. Although that did not happen, but for the intrusive Loopline there is a symmetry about to-day's situation, with the Custom House enclosed within Butt Bridge and Matt Talbot Bridge, so providing the wide river-front promenade illustrated in James Horan's drawing (ill. 54).

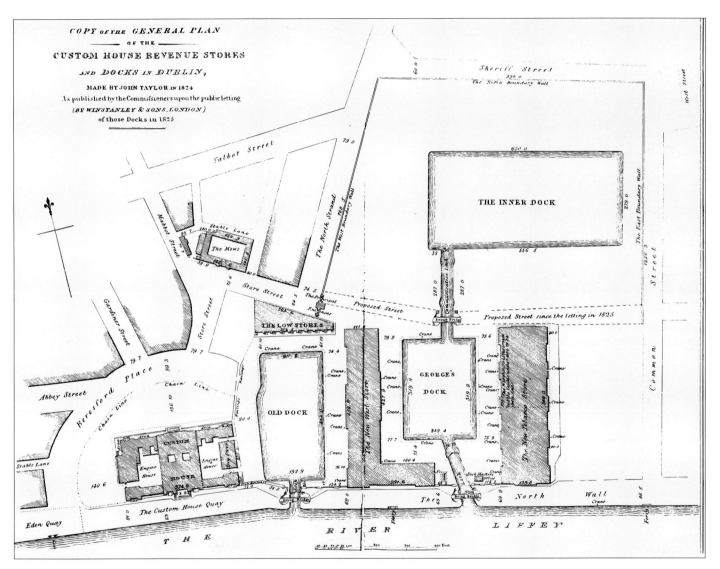

58 Plan (1824) of the Custom House revenue stores and docks

59 Liberty Hall, after bombardment in Easter Week, 1916

(as in illustration 36) but was not built on until 1952, when the curve of Beresford Place was continued round to join Custom House Quay, this new half of the arc (which also extended northwards to join Amiens Street) being named Memorial Road.

Of the buildings contemporary with the Custom House only Gandon's Beresford Place crescent (between Gardiner Street and Store Street) remains. That the crescent was named Beresford Place seems only right and proper: John Beresford, by bringing the new Custom House about, had done more than anyone to make necessary and possible the move of the city to the east, which gave point to all the work of the Wide Street Commissioners.

Illustration 60 is a photograph of the Custom House and Liberty Hall taken at sundown on 11 May 1991, when the work of restoration and conservation of the Custom House was finally completed; illustration 59 also shows Liberty Hall, the pre-

decessor of to-day's building, after it had been shelled in 1916. It was eventually demolished in 1958 to make way for the building we know to-day.

Towards the end of the 1820s Northumberland Buildings were erected on the corner of Eden Quay and Beresford Place. These incorporated the Northumberland Commercial and Family Hotel and, later, Turkish baths, which were entered from Lower Abbey Street. The building was vacated in the late 1800s and fell into disrepair, but in 1912 the Irish Transport and General Workers' Union bought it and renamed it Liberty Hall.

During the 1916 Easter uprising an attempt was made to shell the building by the British gunboat *Helga*, lying downstream from the Loopline Bridge. With more shells hitting the bridge than the building, the bombardment was continued by carriage-mounted guns, brought to the corner of George's Quay and Tara Street.

In 1915 James Connolly installed a printing press in Liberty Hall and it was here, on Easter Sunday, 23 April 1916, that the Proclamation of the Irish Republic was printed.

The War of Independence brought with it more damage to the building and, although it continued to be occupied, by 1956 it had become unsafe and had to be evacuated, and was demolished in 1958.

The new Liberty Hall, a sixteen-storey tower, flanked by conference halls, was designed by Desmond Rea O'Kelly. Its foundation stone was laid in 1962.

The foreword to a booklet on Busaras (designed by Michael Scott, 1905-89), issued shortly after it was opened in 1953, reads: 'In Aras Mhic Dhiarmada – at once the headquarters of the Department of Social Welfare and the city's main bus terminal – Dublin boasts a masterpiece of contemporary architecture

60 (facing page) Liberty Hall and the Custom House, 1991

61 Busaras, taken from the roof of the Custom House, 1997

L connected by the curved scalloped canopy of the main concourse, which echoes the curve of the road. The finest materials were used in construction – handmade bricks on the ground and mezzanine floors, Portland stone facing on the upper floors (a reference to the Custom House opposite), patent glazed windows and mosaic columns in the main concourse.

Busaras was the first major modern building to be erected in the centre of Dublin and quality of workmanship and materials was paramount. Kevin Fox, an architect involved in the project, was later to remark: 'Like Gandon, we were concerned to create a permanent asset, motivated by a respect for architecture in its own right.'

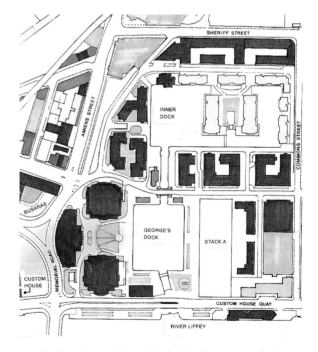

62 Plan by Custom House Docks Development Authority, 1997

and construction which has already taken its place among the great buildings of our time. Work on it was begun in 1946, but changes in governmental policy prevented its completion till seven years later. Despite these delays and the sharply rising cost of materials, the building – one of the largest of its kind in the world – was completed at a cost of just over £1,000,000. Aras Mhic Dhiarmada is named after Sean MacDermott, the Irish leader, executed after the 1916 Rising'.

Busaras (ill. 61) is built on land once occupied by Custom House warehouses (see ill. 36). The island site chosen was a difficult one. It was formed on its two straight sides by Store Street, and on its great curved one by a branch of Memorial Road built to link Beresford Place to Amiens Street. Designed to fit its awkward site, Busaras is L-shaped, with the arms of the

Gandon : "'Pon my word, taking it all in all, that young man didn't do so badly by my Customs House."

63 (above) A *Dublin Opinion* cartoon published when Busaras was built

To-day, the Busaras blends comfortably into the twentieth-century ambience provided by the three adjoining Custom House Docks buildings, AIB Inter-national Centre, IFSC House and La Touche House (ill. 62).

The cartoon of Gandon surveying his Custom House, with Busaras in the background (ill. 63), appeared in the humorous journal *Dublin Opinion* in the 1950s, and was reproduced in *Forty Years of Dublin Opinion* (1961). The artist, W.H. Conn, was a popular contributor to the journal. One critic wrote of his 'meticulously detailed essays in nostalgia', and the editors of the journal (and the book) remarked that 'W.H. Conn's drawings, with their wonderful draughtsmanship and appeal to the mind and the heart, have their special and devoted public among our readers'.

Bravely started in March 1922, by three young men, Arthur Booth, Charles Kelly and Tom Collins, who had no publishing experience, *Dublin Opinion* was an almost immediate success. In 1926, aged only 33, Tom Collins died, but the other two were still the editors forty years later.

The journal was dedicated to the proposition that humour is the safety-valve of a nation, and the lampooning, though shrewd, was never cruel. In their introduction to the 1961 book the editors wrote: 'To one thing we have held from the first: we have written and cartooned for peace in Ireland and everywhere else in the world and, maybe, in a small way, we have helped.'

Certainly this drawing of the Custom House and Busaras reflects Conn's careful attention to detail. Dr Edward McParland wrote, in his booklet on the Custom House, that 'The early Modern Movement in Dublin architecture paid its tribute at Busaras' and, in Conn's drawing, Gandon's ghost appears to agree with him and to look benevolently upon the efforts of 'that young man' Michael Scott. Where, then, does the tribute lie? Perhaps in its horizontality and the way its shorter arm stretches out towards the Custom House, as if acknowledging its debt? Perhaps, also, that the height of the short arm and the Custom House appear equal, as if one is a modern extension of the other, providing a link to the longer, higher arm of the main block of the Busaras at right angles to it? Finally, to quote Kevin Fox again, 'architecture was the object of the exercise and the architect's role was central'; this comment could equally apply to both buildings.

Samuel Frederick Brocas' drawing, *View of the Corn Exchange, Burgh Quay and Custom House* (ill.64), was engraved by his brother Henry for J. Le Petit's *Book of Views of Ireland*, published in 1820. For composition, colour and content it must surely be one of the most attractive pictures in this book.

Although the main emphasis is on the buildings and the scene taking place in the foreground, attention to detail in the depiction of the Custom House in the background is scrupulous: the snarling lion of the coat of arms on the left pavilion can be glimpsed between the rigging of the sailing boat in the foreground; little chimney pots peep out of the urns on the west facade; and the frieze decoration of cattle heads, linked by swags of hide, can be discerned over the main portico.

In spite of the 1800 Act of Union, quayside business seems in no way diminished, and the great mass of ships' masts, and hustle and bustle of activity on the cobbled quayside, testify to the success of the move downriver.

Architecturally, emphasis in this picture is on the Corn Exchange on Burgh Quay (the facade of which can still be seen to-day). It was built in about 1815 and, according to Wright's *Historical Guide* of 1821, the architect was Halpin. This, presumably, was G. Halpin, who was Inspector of Works to the Ballast Board, and who would later become a noted designer of lighthouses. This attribution is not certain, as it has been mooted that Robert Smirke, who is also credited with the Wellington Testimonial obelisk in Phoenix Park, erected at that time, may have been responsible. Which ever it was, he looked long and hard at the west facade of Gandon's Custom House across the river and echoed it in his own.

A structural feature of the Corn Exchange, of great historical interest, was the use of cast iron for the series of hollow columns which carried the large rectangular lantern in the spacious interior of the building. Professor J.W. de Courcy writes in his recent book *The Liffey in Dublin* that the columns, comprising base, shaft and capital, were cast 'in one piece in Coalbrookdale in Shropshire, and transported to Dublin, probably in sailing vessels'. The Halfpenny Bridge, built in 1816, was another example of the early use of cast iron in Dublin.

64 S.F. Brocas, *View of the Corn Exchange, Burgh Quay and Custom House*, 1820

THE CUSTOM HOUSE MOTIF

Items bearing depictions of the Custom House are found to be irresistible by many collectors. Among other things, the motif has featured on beer mugs, art nouveau teapots, posters (Paul Henry designed one for the Great Southern Railways), little enamel embellished copper pill boxes and Victorian sheet music. Rather more seriously, it has not been forgotten on Irish stamps and currency.

In 1991, Dublin was the European City of Culture. To celebrate that year, and also the two-hundredth anniversary of the Custom House, Michael Craig designed a 52p commemorative stamp (ill. 65). He was also responsible for the third (Architectural) and fourth (Treasures of Ireland) definitive series of Irish stamps.

Edward Smyth's riverine heads of the Blackwater, the Lee, the Lagan, the Bann, the Boyne, the Shannon and the Erne were on the backs of the first legal tender notes issued by the Currency Commission in 1928, and Anna Livia, in her turn, can be seen on the back of the current Irish £10 bank note, designed by Robert Ballagh (ill. 66). Consolidated bank notes were introduced by the Currency Commission in 1929, in an effort to standardize design of private bank notes (before 1929 five of the Associated Banks, the National, the Northern, the Ulster, the Bank of Ireland and the Provincial, had their own designs). The issue was terminated on 31 December 1953. These Consolidated bank notes were issued in denominations of £1, £5, £10, £50 and £100, all with the same picture on the front (a farmer ploughing his field, hence the name 'Ploughman's' note (ill. 67), but with a different design for each value on the back, set into an elaborate scalloped frame.

The Custom House was depicted on the back of the £1 note (ill. 68) and is of interest from an architectural point of view. The Consolidated notes were not issued until 1929 so, although we would expect to see the Loopline Bridge and the lower profile of the earlier Liberty Hall, we would certainly not expect to see the four statues still in place over the main portico; by this date, in their sorry dismembered state, they had already been lurking for some years in the Custom House grounds. Obviously the Currency Commission artist, E.L. Lawrenson, preferred to hark back to the good old days, before the 1921 fire.

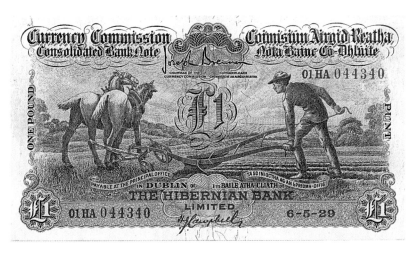

65 Front of the £1 Consolidated bank note, 1929

67 Design of the current £10 note

66 Back of the £1 Consolidated bank note, 1929

68 1991 postage stamp

69 A nurse on Nelson Pillar : detail of a collage photographed by Fr Browne

Recognizable in this skillfully constructed montage are the former Houses of Parliament (now the Bank of Ireland), the Four Courts, the GPO and, dominating them all, with not only its own cupola but Dublin Castle's Record Tower and Christchurch Cathedral erupting from its roof, the Custom House. A closer inspection of the pillar in the foreground reveals that Nelson has been replaced on his column by one of the nurses responsible for drawing the Sweepstake tickets (ill. 69).

The Jesuit priest Father Francis Mary Browne (1880-1960) was an active photographer from his boyhood days. His work enabled him to travel the world and he left a precious legacy of over 40,000 negatives (approximately 3,500 of Dublin), recording the events, places and, most importantly, people, who had captured his interest throughout his long life.

In the 1930s the Jesuits took over Emo Court, which was designed by James Gandon for Lord Carlow, first Earl of Portarlington, in the 1780s. Here, with special blinds and curtains, Father Browne's bedroom doubled up as a dark room, to which it could be converted within seconds. There were often occasions when members of his community were denied access to the bathroom, which not only stank of chemicals but where the bath was frequently full of films undergoing a final wash!

Although Father Browne never managed to get to America, in April 1912 his uncle, Robert Browne, the Bishop of Cloyne, who knew of his interest in transatlantic liners, made him a present of the first two legs of a voyage on an America-bound ship. He was among those who boarded the liner at Southampton, which then sailed on to Cherbourg to collect more passengers, before continuing to Queenstown (now Cobh), in Cork, the last port of call before America. Father Browne made American friends on board, who invited him to be their guest on the final leg of the journey, but this was not allowed by his Provincial and he reluctantly disembarked at Cork. The name of the liner was the *Titanic*!

If the building on the right hand side of the Father Browne photograph (ill. 70), clearly recognizable as the Mansion House, had been omitted, together with the tall building on the left, any bewilderment felt by the viewer would have been understandable. Those of us who were around in the days of Nelson's Pillar would have wondered why we had never noticed this huge white building, a hybrid of styles and periods of architecture, standing right beside the pillar. But the Mansion House was not omitted and so we realise that we are looking at a mock-up of some of Dublin's most beautiful buildings which, in fact, was assembled as part of a pageant outside the Mansion House in 1938, to promote the Irish Hospitals Sweepstakes.

70 Fr Browne's collage for the Irish Hospitals Sweepstakes pageant, 1938

SEVEN MORE VIEWS

This book ends with a selection of seven illustrations of the Custom House in a variety of media. By now, there is little new to tell; but it is hoped that, between them, they will reinforce and draw together all the points made so far.

The photograph shown in illustration 71) is the earliest known of the Custom House. It was taken in 1843, from Burgh Quay, and has been attributed to the Reverend Calvert Jones. At this date Butt Bridge and the Loopline have yet to be built and so the ships are berthed upriver as far as Carlisle Bridge. As in the James Hore paintings (ills. 24 & 25), the Custom House can be seen through a forest of masts, as can the now familiar Northumberland Buildings, on the corner of Eden Quay and Beresford Place, and between them a range of buildings which we know from Hore's painting was of red brick and, like Northumberland Buildings (which, of course, was to become Liberty Hall) would be demolished in the fullness of time.

The foreground is hard to make out but beside a small horse-drawn dray a group of people are clustered in the bottom right hand corner, beside the quay wall. Are we looking at dyslexic graffiti on that wall or do these letters concern some dockside activity? Perhaps one of the nicest touches in this photograph is the reflection of the wheel and spokes of the dray, lying at the feet of the two seated men.

As for the Custom House itself, the pre-fire skyline profile has, by now, become familiar, with its Portland stone cupola and a full complement of statues and chimneys.

The tiny little topographical print reproduced on pages 86-87 was found by the picture researcher in a small book *Views in Ireland* published by Nelson & Sons *c.*1871 and confirms that 'Small is beautiful'. Once more, almost everything in it will be familiar. The Custom House is drawn with infinite care, right down to the swags on the chimney urns (from which, again, we see chimney pots emerging) and on the plinth beneath the statue of Commerce atop the dome. Here again are the piers and iron railings enclosing the Old Dock. This print clearly shows that there is a lamp on top of each pier and further examination of Mares' photograph (ill. 28) reveals that, indeed, they are there as well.

The detail of the cluttered quayside activity repays examination under a magnifying glass, showing such things as the carefully drawn harness of the paired horses in the foreground, the fashionable clothes of the people who appear to be promenading on the pavement in front of the Custom House and, what has not been seen in other pictures (except for the ramp in Berger's *Marine View* (ill. 5), a gangplank propped against the side of the

71 (facing page) An early (1843) photograph by Calvert Jones

72 *The Liffey, Custom House and Eden Quay*, a c.1870 print published by Nelson & Sons

sailing ship moored alongside the quay while loading or unloading is taking place. Because of lack of space at the Custom House Quay, ships could only moor alongside while dealing with their cargoes. Until their turn came they moored in line on George's Quay opposite, at right angles to it, attached to the quay by the bow of the boat (hence the sailors' bowline knot).

The large sailing ship, just off centre, is riding high in the water, which means she is empty of cargo. She is either being towed back out to sea by the little tug (we can see where the water is churning from her paddles) or, perhaps, to pick up another cargo. Tugs were much in use at this time to tow the large sailing ships, which could not proceed so far upriver under sail and so were unable to manoeuvre their own way around.

This print gives a particularly clear view of Northumberland Buildings and those adjoining them on Eden Quay, and we can also see Gandon's Carlisle Bridge with the sailing ships moored right up to it, and the whole wide scene of river, ships and Custom House is thrown into sharp relief by the brilliant blue sky.

Robert Mannix's painting (ill. 73) is probably one of the most interesting in the book, encapsulating, as it does, so many aspects of the life which went on around and about the Custom House in the early 1880s, and of the Custom House itself. It is a carefully painted study where attention has been given to every smallest detail, whether of ships' rigging, quayside activities or the architecture of the Custom House.

Mannix has chosen to illustrate the south-west pavilion. Unlike Malton (ill. 9), who hides this face in shadow (perhaps

to give the illusion that the building was even more glorious than it is, and constructed entirely in Portland stone) Mannix clearly shows that the main walling on this side of the building is of granite. He strongly contrasts this more sombre stone with the gleaming Portland stone quoins (dressed stones at the corners of buildings), cornice and balustrade, string course, architraves and stonecarving which beautify the building.

The date of the painting is 1883. Had it been painted ten years later we would not have seen Dean & Woodward's

obelisk-like drinking fountain standing in the foreground, in Beresford Place, for it was removed to make way for the Loopline railway bridge of 1891. Although it is not shown in this picture, the old Butt (Swivel) Bridge is already in situ, there since 1879. The photograph of the swivel bridge (ill. 50) would have been taken around the time this picture was painted; in it the drinking fountain, flagpole and street light in the foreground of Mannix's painting can all be seen.

David Slattery, when working on the Custom House restoration, also trusted Mannix's depiction for, when it came to painting the clock faces in the cupola, the shade of blue was chosen to match that in the picture.

The Custom House Quay is as cluttered and busy as ever with dockside activity, confirming that its use was not reserved for Guinness boats alone, although in the right corner of the painting we can see a Guinness barge, with its distinctive red and black funnel, laden with casks.

Rose Barton's painting of the Departure of the 4th Dragoon Guards from the Custom House Quay in 1891 (ill. 46) has already been discussed, and provides an interesting contrast with her view of the Custom House (overleaf) seen from George's Quay. While the Dragoon Guards picture is full of people, alive with the bustle of departure, this is calmer and more gentle, with the components merging softly into each other.

The date of this painting is uncertain. It was exhibited at the Royal Society of Painters in Water-Colours in 1927 under the title *The Custom House, Dublin, before the Rebellion* and, sure enough, we can recognise the building in its pre-1921 state. It could, therefore, have been an earlier painting which she had not exhibited before, or perhaps she painted it later from her pre-1921 sketches. Either way, it is delightful. George's Quay,

and the dark hulls of the ships moored alongside it, contrast with the luminous, warm, pinky-mauve colours of the rest of the picture. Mercifully, the Loopline Bridge has been absorbed into the haze of the horizon and the Custom House is silhouetted against the wide lemon sky, while its reflection, and those of the boats moored alongside (one of them a Guinness boat?), shivers in the rippling water.

In 1966 *The Last of the Arklow Schooners* (ill. 75) was one of fifty in Flora Mitchell's book *Vanishing Dublin*, where each watercolour drawing was reproduced in colour, with a short accompanying commentary. Her commentary, in this case, noted that the russet sails and black hulls of the Arklow schooners were a common sight for fifty years or more, as they lay alongside Butt Bridge, with the Custom House as a background across the river.

The date of the painting is uncertain as Gilligan, in his *History of the Port of Dublin*, writes that the Arklow fleet was gone by 1961, and the day of the coasting sailing vessel with it. Arklow sailing ships hold a proud place in Irish maritime history, many being built in the famous Tyrrell shipyard. It is on record that the last two commercial sailing vessels, of 121 and 136 tonnes, were built by John Tyrrell & Sons at Arklow in 1920-22. The most common cargoes for Irish coastal and cross-channel runs were coal, china clay, grain, sand, bricks, malt and oats.

Flora Mitchell was born in America but came to Europe at an early age. In 1910 she was a student at the Dublin Metropolitan School of Art and it was here that she developed her technique of making meticulous pencil sketches from life, which she subsequently went over with Indian ink and then filled in with watercolour. She exhibited regularly in Dublin and every year at the Royal Hibernian Academy between 1957 and 1970. In 1930 she married a great-grandson of the founder

73 (facing page) Robert Mannix, *The Port of Dublin and Custom House*, 1883

Custom House
Dublin
Rose Barton.

74 (facing page) Rose Barton, *The Custom House before the Rebellion*

75 Flora Mitchell, *The Last of the Arklow Schooners*, c.1966

76 Alethea Garstin, *Guinness's Boat*

of the Jameson's distillery firm and was widowed thirty years before her own death, in Killiney, Co. Dublin, on 13 April 1973.

Alethea Garstin (1894-1978) has taken the same theme for her painting, *Guinness's Boat* (ill. 76), as did the photographer Joachim Gerstenberg, (see ill. 47), with the Custom House providing a backdrop for one of the Guinness sea-going vessels and a barge.

Garstin's approach in this painting is *alla prima*. The paint has been laid on directly with no attempt made to rework a palette limited to three colours. The unprimed panel is allowed to show through extensively in the composition to great effect.

Alethea Garstin was born in Penzance, daughter of the artist Norman Garstin, with whom, in company with his pupils, she went on sketching holidays from an early age. She took up painting at the age of sixteen, her father being her only teacher, and at the age of eighteen had her first picture accepted for the Royal Academy. She travelled widely and, through her close artistic friendship with Morland Lewis, a pupil of Walter Sickert, absorbed something of Sickert's teachings.

Always preferring to work on a small scale and *en plein air*, Alethea, like her father, had no theory on painting. Her father, in an interview in 1907, was quoted as saying 'My chief theory on painting is not to have a theory. Painting is a purely personal matter.'

The last image in the book (ill. 77), was drawn in September 1991. The artist has taken for his subject just one section of the Custom House, the front portico, zooming in on its monumentality as a photographer might with his special lens, and it took him just ten minutes to draw, standing up and leaning against the parapet of the Matt Talbot Bridge!

The human story behind this drawing is one of poignancy, excitement and mystery. It was executed by Stephen Wiltshire,

77 Stephen Wiltshire, drawing, 1991

when on a visit to Dublin sponsored by the Irish Society for Autism. Stephen was born on 24 April 1974, in London, to West Indian parents. He was diagnosed as being autistic when he was three and, until he was five, lived in his own sad, lonely world, having no language, unable to make relationships and prone to uncontrolled tantrums.

Things began to look up for him when he was five and went to Queensmill School in London, where his teacher, Chris Marris, discovered his aptitude for drawing; his first word was 'paper'. Since then his drawing talent has known no bounds, especially where architecture and cityscapes are concerned. He has an intuitive grasp of perspective and an astonishing visual memory as, having looked at a building for a short time, he can go away and produce a faithful drawing of it some time later.

Now 22, Stephen is a full-time student at City & Guilds London Art School, pursuing a three-year degree course in drawing and painting. He is the first autistic artistic savant in Britain to have been accepted by an art school. Behind him lies a blazing trail of publications of his work, television interviews, exhibitions and scholarships. Initially the focus of attention on Stephen's art obscured his extraordinary musical skills; he is pitch perfect, can identify any key and has become a natural musical performer.

Stephen will probably always be incapable of independent existence, and in need of special understanding, support and care, and so his achievements seem all the more astounding. Sir Robin Philipson, past-President of the Royal Scottish Academy, wrote on the cover of one of Stephen's published collections of drawings: 'I have never stood so much in awe of a marvellous, mysterious gift. This boy is enormously blessed with a profoundly deep form of communication that touches us all - This is an achievement to be celebrated and nurtured'.

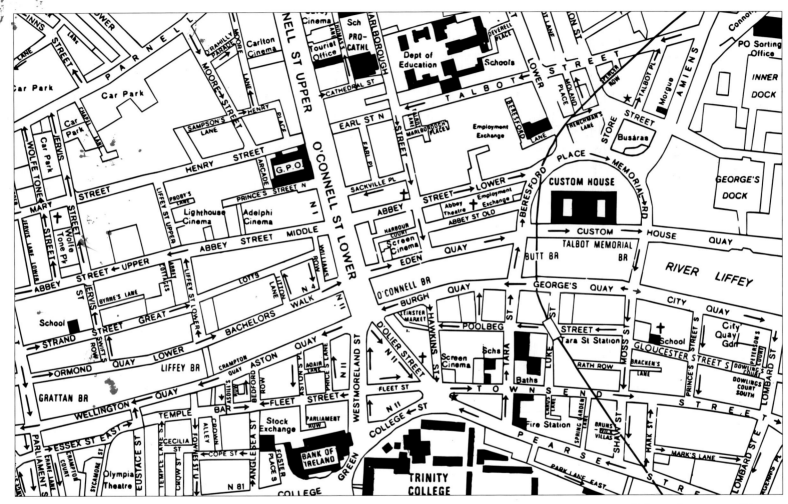

78 1992 Ordnance Survey map of the area surrounding the Custom House